the remodeler's

MARKETING
PowerPak

Linda Case
Victoria Downing

Remodelers
ADVANTAGE®

Fulton, Maryland

the remodeler's
MARKETING
PowerPak

By Linda Case and Victoria Downing

Published by
Remodelers
ADVANTAGE®

REMODELERS ADVANTAGE, INC.
8504 Edenton Road
Fulton, MD 20759 U.S.A.
www.RemodelersAdvantage.com

Copyright © 2004 by Linda Case and Victoria Downing
First Printing 1995

Printed in the United States of America.
Library of Congress Control Number 2003115321

ISBN: 0964858770

Cover & book design by Cristina Diez de Medina, *A Scribbler's Press Ltd.*

thank you!

Thanks to those generous remodelers and experts who allowed us to tell their stories. Their contributions made this book vibrant, entertaining and most importantly, genuine:

PATRICK CROWLEY, PATRICK M. CROWLEY, INC. • THOMAS BUCKBOROUGH, THOMAS E. BUCKBOROUGH & ASSOCIATES • DALE NIKULA, ENCORE CONSTRUCTION, INC. • TOM AND TRISH SCHROEDER, SCHROEDER DESIGN/BUILD • GARY AND CRAIG DEIMLER, DEIMLER & SONS CONSTRUCTION • GARY AND JANE STOKES, ADR BUILDERS, LTD. • GENO BENVENUTI, BENVENUTI & STEIN, INC. • PATTI MCDANIEL, BOARDWALK BUILDERS, INC. • JONAS CARNEMARK, CARNEMARK SYSTEMS + DESIGN INC. • NINA AND PAUL WINANS, WINANS CONSTRUCTION, INC. • DAVID BRYAN, BLACKDOG BUILDERS, INC. • TERRY STREICH AND GARY WELTON, SILVER BULLET DESIGN & BUILD, INC. • GREGG JOHNSON AND BRUCE JOHNSON, LEE KIMBALL KITCHENS, INC. • DAVID AND KAREN MERRILL, MERRILL CONTRACTING & REMODELING • SALVATORE FERRO AND CARL HYMAN, ALURE HOME IMPROVEMENT • BOB FLEMING, CLASSIC REMODELING & CONSTRUCTION, INC. • JAY CONRAD LEVINSON, *GUERRILLA MARKETING SERIES* • JERRY AND ANN KELLY, ABBEY ROAD CONSTRUCTION • JOHN MURPHY, MURPHY BROS. BUILDING & REMODELING CO. • SUE AND BOB MCDOWELL, MCDOWELL, INC. OF ST. CHARLES • JEB BREITHAUB, JEB DESIGN/BUILD • BOB DUBREE, CREATIVE CONTRACTING INC. • CHAD CARPENTER AND KAREN DOWD-CARPENTER, POTOMAC BUILDERS, INC. • GREGORY A. ANTONIOLI, OUT OF THE WOODS CONSTRUCTION • MARK AND THERESA SWIMME, SWIMME & SON BUILDING CONTRACTORS, INC. • KELLY & ERICH EGGERS AND MICHAEL & JOAN CORDONNIER, REMODELING DESIGNS, INC. • BOB CONNELLY AND MELISSA CONNELLY, R.L. CONNELLY & COMPANY, INC. • ADAM HELFMAN, FAIRWAY CONSTRUCTION COMPANY • PAMELA STANMIRE, ASTRO E-DESIGN SOLUTIONS • LARRY PARRISH, PARRISH CONSTRUCTION CO. • JEFFREY TITUS, TITUS BUILT, L.L.C.

It's been said that many hands make light work, and every book—while not light work—is the result of the collaboration of many hands and minds. This book benefits greatly from the great eye for graphics, page composition and font selection provided by Cristina Diez de Medina, A Scribbler's Press Ltd.; from careful and caring editing and final reading of Jill Tunick, Jill Tunick and Associates; and from the support of Christa Blake, Remodelers Advantage Inc., who helped to mother its birth.

All of us hope that it has just the right answers for you and that the ideas and illustrations will lead you to the uniquely successful generation of the quality prospects that you deserve.

contents

part three

INCREASING REPEAT BUSINESS AND REFERRAL LEADS

part four

REACHING OUT TO TARGETED PROSPECTS

part five

part six

part seven

resources

introduction

Why Is Marketing So Important?

Welcome to the updated version of our *Remodeler's Marketing PowerPak,* which was originally published in 1995. In this book you'll again find time-tested principles of successful marketing along with dozens of real-life examples from remodelers who have made their marketing work. Whether your company is small or large, the marketing tools in this book will help you increase your company's visibility and produce quality leads throughout this year...and every year.

One remodeler (who used minimal marketing) recently said to us, "This marketing stuff is overrated!" We heartily disagree. Marketing is an essential part of running a successful business. It's the fuel that powers your company machine and it can affect many areas of your business. Here are some examples.

An effective marketing/lead generation program will:

- Lessen the effects of the market's highs and lows by providing a **steady flow of leads** throughout the year.
- Produce quality leads that let you pick and choose the **projects that you want** to work on.
- Attract the **types of customers** you enjoy working with.
- **Reposition** your company so you're known in the community for new or expanded services.
- **Pre-sell your company**, making the sales process easier and less stressful.

▸ Lastly, and probably most importantly, an effective marketing program will **position** your company in such a way that your prospects will be willing to pay a professional fee for your services—helping you **sell value,** not price.

An effective lead generation program focuses on quality, not quantity. You want the right leads, for the right job, at the right price. Because your time is so valuable, you must concentrate on targeted jobs and avoid wasting time on prospective customers who aren't a good fit for the prices you demand or the services you offer.

Every company does marketing; that's because every company has a public side. However if you're not guiding that marketing effort, you're depending on the market to keep your company viable. Yes, word-of-mouth referrals can help a great deal, but to be highly profitable or to grow your company, you must have a productive lead generation program in place.

An effective program is more than one or two simple marketing activities. The most successful programs incorporate several marketing tactics simultaneously. In this *Marketing PowerPak*, you'll find dozens of ready-to-use ideas that have worked for thousands of remodelers across the country. They can work for you too. Of course, you won't use every one—just those that will help you reach your company goals.

Let's get started.

part one

STARTING AT THE BEGINNING

WHAT DO YOU WANT TO ACCOMPLISH?

All too often, business owners want to start their marketing programs immediately. They send messages out into the world before they've developed goals for their programs. But just like preplanning a remodeling project ensures its successful completion, developing your business and marketing goals is critical for creating the right lead generation program. Advanced planning and setting objectives makes the difference between aiming at something in the sight of a highly accurate rifle or just hoping to hit the target with the broad spray of a shotgun—if you get lucky.

Careful aim has two important benefits in marketing:

▶ You'll invest much less money in your marketing program because you're not wasting dollars on disorganized efforts.

▶ The leads you generate with a targeted program are of higher quality because they fit your definition of your targeted prospect. Therefore, these leads are easier to sell.

In this section, we'll ask you to do some hard thinking about your business as you complete an array of exercises. Taking the time to thoughtfully complete this section will help you choose the right direction for your marketing efforts.

So let's start our planning!

WHAT ARE YOUR MARKETING GOALS?

Check all that apply:

☐ Increase volume (from _____ to _____)

☐ Sell at higher prices

☐ Make selling easier

☐ Increase referrals and repeat business

☐ Raise job size

☐ Target a specific niche

☐ Attract a new kind of customer

☐ Promote a new product or service

☐ Increase market awareness

☐ Other _____

ANALYZE THE COMPANY

Where are you today? Complete a Strengths, Weaknesses, Opportunities, and Threats (SWOT) Analysis:

Strengths. What does your company bring to the marketplace that is better or different than what any other company offers?

_____

_____

_____

Weaknesses. In what areas do you need improvement? Are there particulars about your company that could be seen as detrimental?

_____

_____

_____

Opportunities. What marketplace events and trends could uncover business opportunities for you? Examples: a new product development, new niche marketing development.

_____

_____

_____

Threats. What situation(s) or possible event(s) could pose a risk to the business? Examples: the defection of a long-term employee, the possible illness or death of a principal, or a large competitor entering the marketplace.

_____

_____

_____

MARKETING SUCCESS FORMULA:
IT'S A NUMBERS GAME!

1. What volume/revenue would you like to reach next year?

_____

2. What is your average job size? _____

Be sure you have a true reading of your average job size. Owners often have a "gut feel" for this information but when the numbers are actually analyzed, many discover to their chagrin that their average job size is actually quite a bit smaller. This could significantly impact your marketing strategy.

3. Number of jobs to be sold:

Divide volume/revenue (exercise 1) by the average job size (exercise 2).

4. Closing ratio for raw leads: one sale for every _____
        leads the company receives.

How many leads must come in before you close a sale? These should be "raw" leads, meaning each call that comes in, whether or not it turns out to be a good lead for the company. If you need 10 leads to close one sale, your closing ratio is 10:1. This statistic helps you identify which marketing tactics are producing the most leads and the highest quality (prospects more likely to buy) leads.

5. Total leads needed this year:

Multiply the number of jobs to be sold (exercise 3) by the closing ratio number (exercise 4).

6. Total leads needed each month:

Divide the annual leads needed (exercise 5) by 12.

7. Closing ratio for qualified leads: one sale for every _____
        leads the company receives that is deemed worthy of an appointment
        with the prospect.

Qualified leads are those leads that you determine, through qualifying, are worth the time and energy investment for a company representative to pursue. In other words, you feel you have a good chance of closing the job and the project fits your company's guidelines for a good job.

8. Total qualified leads needed this year: _____

Multiply the number of jobs to be sold (exercise 3) by the closing ratio number (exercise 7).

9. Total qualified leads needed each month: _____

Divide the annual qualified leads needed (exercise 8) by 12.

WHERE IS YOUR BUSINESS COMING FROM NOW?

Review last year's leads to determine the lead source. Complete the form below:

From

Repeat customers	_____ %
Referrals from previous customers	_____ %
Referrals from other sources	_____ %
Job site marketing	_____ %
Home/mall shows	_____ %
Direct mail	_____ %
Newsletters	_____ %
Truck signage	_____ %
Publicity	_____ %
Web site	_____ %
Yellow Pages	_____ %
Newspaper ads	_____ %
Magazine ads	_____ %
Radio commercials	_____ %
Television commercials	_____ %

Other lead sources:

_____ %

_____ %

_____ %

PROJECT SWEET SPOT:
THE BEST KINDS OF JOBS FOR YOUR COMPANY

Profile the last 20 jobs you've completed and look at the gross profit each of them generated. Can you identify certain types of jobs that deliver consistently higher profits to the company? Determine why this is so. Once you determine the most profitable jobs, think about the jobs you most enjoy doing. Do they match? If not, spend some time thinking about what you want from your company.

Complete the following: *The best kind of job for my company is:*

Size: $ _____

Type: _____

Style, if applicable   _____

Gross profit range: _____%

Other: _____

CHOOSING A PROFITABLE, ENJOYABLE NICHE

Too many people try to be everything to everybody, and it just doesn't work. We recommend that you identify areas of specialization—niches—to work in. Working in a niche offers plenty of advantages:

▸ By limiting your work to one niche, you'll discover that you have **less direct competition** than you would if you tried to do it all. Just look in the *Yellow Pages* and count all of the generalists you could be competing against. However, if you specialize in historic homes, you'd find there are dramatically fewer companies sharing your specialty. You may come into contact with new and inexperienced contractors on one or two jobs within your niche, but they frequently limp away whimpering because they don't have the knowledge or skills to do the job right.

- Since you'll be concentrating your generalized skills on a specific area of remodeling, you'll **quickly become a technique and product knowledge expert** in your field. People will pay more for that expertise.

- Your crews will learn the best ways to handle the details of one kind of work, making them **faster and more efficient.** This means you can do the work more quickly and earn more profits on each job.

- Once you've begun to be known in your niche, you'll **gain referrals** from within that specialized community.

- A niche serves a confined market so it's not necessary—or desirable—to market, to a broad audience. This means you're able **to spend your resources more effectively** by targeting just those people who need the services you offer.

A Company Niche can be Defined by:

- **Type of service you offer**. For example, this might be design/build or insurance restoration.

- **Type of property you like to work on.** Do you enjoy historic renovation or prefer retrofitting retail space?

- **Type of work that your company does.** Some remodeling companies specialize in creating additions on two-story colonial buildings while others only handle interior work, such as kitchens and baths.

- **Geographic area.** Some remodelers have customers all over a metropolitan area; some only accept work in specific districts.

- **Products.** You could specialize in one type of window or siding, or perhaps join a franchise that represents one type of product.

- Size of your jobs. Do you like to do small jobs that can be completed in a week or less, or would you rather do larger, more complex projects?

- Clientele you prefer to work for. Do you like to do work for wealthy clients? It's not for everyone. Some remodelers prefer working for middle-class, senior, or disabled people.

Locating your business in a rural, less densely populated area may force you to stay more generalized because the market can't support a specialist. However, urban and suburban areas usually provide enough prospects to successfully support a specialized niche.

Many successful remodelers are characterized by the fact that they have positioned their companies to serve a specialized niche. All of their marketing—image, public relations, advertising, and networking—is targeted to serve that niche. The way you position your company is crucial and far from arbitrary. There are thousands of different platforms your business can stand on for increased value. When you find a niche, stop and think about how to go after more of that specific work. Who buys that work and how can you reach them? Are there publications or conferences that serve this specific market?

Targeting a well-defined niche means you can compete on the basis of value, not price. To make the most of your potential, you must have a clear idea of what your company's niche is and then market that specialty.

 WHAT'S YOUR COMPANY'S NICHE?

Complete this sentence as clearly and concisely as possible:

Our company's niche is: _____

⬚ STREET SMARTS

Pat Crowley is the president of Patrick M. Crowley, Inc., in Johnston, R.I., a thriving business that has been working exclusively for dentists since 1990. The company's marketing positions it as an expert in the intricacies of remodeling dentists' offices, and backs that claim up with the extensive knowledge Pat has gained through the years. The company doesn't just claim to be tops in its field; it demonstrates that fact from the very first customer contact. Very few companies can compete with Patrick M. Crowley, Inc., and dentists are willing to pay more for the skill the company brings to the table. That's the beauty of a niche!

WHERE DO YOU WANT TO BE IN THE FUTURE?

Since your marketing can help mold your company into a tool to deliver on your personal goals, it's important to think about the future as you devise your marketing strategies. To help you do this, answer the following questions:

1. **What do I want my business to look like in five years?**

   _____

   _____

2. **How big will my business be?**

   _____

   _____

3. **What will my role in the business be?**

   _____

   _____

4. **What services will I offer? (Design, construction, etc.)**

   _____

   _____

5. **Whom else do I want to sell my services to? Why?**

   _____

   _____

6. **If I walked up to someone in my town five years from now and asked what they know about my company, what would I like them to say?**

   _____

   _____

7. **How far am I today from achieving what I want?**

   _____

   _____

ANALYZE THE CUSTOMER

Review your last 20 clients and try to determine if similarities exist. Identifying these similarities will help you target like-minded clients. If you want to move toward a different type of client, review your client list for those who fit the desired profile. If you want to change clientele altogether, create a profile to describe that ideal client.

Complete the list below. Although many of the following characteristics are oriented toward residential clients, they can be modified for commercial or business-to-business buyers.

Client Demographics

Average age: _____

Household income: _____

Two income earners or one? _____

Professional or blue collar? _____

Family size: _____

Marital status: _____

Ethnicity: _____

Level of education: _____

Top three client professions:

1. _____

2. _____

3. _____

Location/neighborhood.

Name the top three or four locations for your top customers.

1. _____

2. _____

3. _____

Age of home: _____

Are you helping them solve specific problems?
What are these issues?

_____

_____

_____

ANALYZE THE COMPETITION

Knowledge is strength and the more information you have about your competitors, the easier it will be to sell against them. Understanding the benefits your company brings to the table vs. what your competitors offer can give you a huge advantage. Some remodelers say, "I don't care what my competitors do. I'm not afraid of them." But market intellingence isn't about fear—it's about increasing your knowledge base to give you power in the selling situation.

Complete this exercise for each of your top five competitors:

Volume _____

Location _____

Number of employees _____

Years in business _____

Differences in business model _____
(Uses more subs? Family business? Works with architects?)

_____

_____

_____

_____

_____

Differences in clientele

To gather this information

▸ Read their marketing information.

▸ Visit their web sites.

▸ Talk to them. Many of your competitors will be surprisingly open.

_____

_____

_____

YOUR MARKETING MESSAGE

Why should people buy from you instead of your competitors? What makes your company different? Why is your company a better choice?

Pretend you're eavesdropping on a conversation your clients are having with friends. They've said that they are delighted with your work and the way you go about your business. You are, to your customers, exactly what they want you to be. That's wonderful! But why do they feel that way? Fill in the blanks in the conversation:

They are asked:

"What is it that makes (your company name) so good?"

_____

_____

_____

"What do you especially value about the way (your company name) does the job?"

_____

_____

_____

"What do you especially value about the way they treat you?"

_____

_____

_____

"What are they always careful to do?"

_____

_____

_____

"What are they always careful not to do?"

_____

_____

_____

FEATURES AND BENEFITS

In order of importance, list five features your company offers to your customers that makes a difference to them. Features might be the length of time your company has been in business, your central location, the fact that your carpenters are employees (not subcontractors), or many other things.

Features

1. _____
2. _____
3. _____
4. _____
5. _____

Now translate these features into benefits. Put yourself in your customers' shoes and say to yourself, "Why should I care? What does that mean to me?"

For example, your customers should care that you've been in business for 15 years because your company is experienced, established, and is likely to still be in business if your customers have a problem or need in the future. It means you have plenty of happy customers throughout the community who will attest to your skill and quality. It means you'll be there to handle warranty callbacks that might arise after the job is completed—just as you've been there for previous customers over the years.

Benefits

1. _____
2. _____
3. _____
4. _____
5. _____

Stress these benefits in all of your marketing materials. Customers don't care about features; they care about benefits! All marketing must answer the customer's question "What's in it for me?"

HOW MUCH SHOULD YOU SPEND?

We've all heard the saying, "It takes money to make money." In marketing, it takes money to generate leads. By spending your dollars on marketing, you're investing in the future of your business. You're betting that the lead generation dollars you spend will create a consistent flow of quality leads that will translate into more profits and more success for your company.

For a small company just starting to market, it's frightening to take hard-earned dollars and spend them, hoping you'll get a return. By following the guidelines in this book and beginning with the least risky tactics, you can be comfortable that your marketing will pay off.

Experience shows that typical marketing budgets for full-line remodeling companies are in the range of 2–5% of the projected yearly volume. The end of that range you need depends on your average job size. If job sizes are small or if you are planning to grow the company, you may need the full 5%. If your company works in the rarefied niche of very large projects (over $150,000), and has a stable volume level, you will rarely need more than a 1–2% budget to put together a very effective program.

Specialty or single-line remodeling companies typically budget between 10%–15% of projected volume for marketing. Because their individual job sizes are smaller, specialty companies must spend more on marketing because they need a much higher quantity of leads than most full-line companies do.

Your marketing budget should include:
▸ Design of materials
▸ Printing
▸ Postage
▸ Photography
▸ Uniforms

- Job site signs
- Brochures
- Media costs
- Membership dues for networking organizations
- Web site development and maintenance
- Anything else created to help your company generate leads

While this amount of money may sound high, remember that it includes the cost of the personnel to implement the program. So if you're in charge of the marketing efforts and you spend 25% of your time managing it, 25% of your salary should be applied to the marketing budget.

When you think of implementing your marketing program, think of a scale that represents your total marketing resources. One side of that scale is piled with your money and the other holds hours of your time. You have to decide which you'd rather spend—time or money—to start the program and keep it going. You can implement effective tactics with less cash outlay by spending more of your time, or you can use your time elsewhere and spend money for someone to help you market. But you must choose one or the other.

MARKETING RESOURCES

When considering how to spend these limited marketing resources, we recommend following the guidelines set by Jay Conrad Levinson in his book, *Guerrilla Marketing:*

▸ Spend **60%** of your marketing resources on your **Circle of Influence.** Your Circle of Influence includes previous customers and anyone who can potentially refer business to your company, such as your accountant, lawyer, real estate agents or other business or personal associates. It should include suppliers and subcontractors as well. These people are the source of the best leads you have available: referrals and repeat business.

▸ Spend **30%** of your marketing investment on your **prospects**—those people who have some reason to be possible buyers. Prospects could be neighbors surrounding job sites, homeowners in a particular neighborhood, or people with homes of a certain age. When looking for prospects, think about the types of people that you're working for now. Where would you find more people just like them?

- Spend **10%** of your resources to reach everyone in your market area, **the Universe.** This could be done with newspaper or radio advertising, for example. We recommend dedicating such a small amount to this group because you'll reach many people, but few will be your top prospects.

YOUR LEAD GENERATION BUDGET

Complete the following statements:

In the coming year, I want my company sales volume to be $ _____ .

Therefore, my marketing budget for the coming year will be _____ %

of this expected sales volume, or $ _____ .

WHO WILL GET IT DONE?

You probably wear many hats—and that usually translates into not having enough time to do everything. We've found that marketing is often one of the first things to be dropped from the owner's long list of responsibilities. When this happens, the stream of incoming leads can dry up, leaving the company in a real bind. Because it can take up to six months for a new marketing program to produce dependable leads, it's important that your marketing program be implemented consistently.

IN-HOUSE VS. SUBCONTRACTING

So what do you do when time is tight? Well, since you understand and agree that marketing is a critical part of your business, you can do like many others and make time in your current schedule for this high-priority task. Or you can hire someone to handle parts of the program. This person could be someone already in your office who has extra time that can be devoted to implementing the marketing. Or it could be a part-time employee—or subcontractor—hired specifically for this purpose. A local university student majoring in marketing might be an excellent choice. Or you could hire a marketing consultant to help with specific parts of the marketing program while you handle the rest.

If you decide to assign the responsibility for implementing your lead generation program to someone on your staff, be sure that person is enthusiastic about the addition of this new responsibility and has a good marketing mindset. This means he or she believes in the benefits that marketing brings to the company, understands basic marketing principles, and is constantly looking for creative ways to attract prospects.

Whichever direction you choose, you as the owner should remain very involved in the planning stages. No one knows the company as well as you do, so your input is critical for designing a program that will help you reach your goals. If you do use an outside resource to implement the program, ask for regular reports on each tactic's results so you can decide which efforts are worth a continued investment and which should be dropped.

 ## YOUR MARKETING MANAGER

The person who will be responsible for implementing this marketing program is: _____

CREATING YOUR MARKETING TEAM

In addition to the company representative who will be implementing the program, you'll also be working with a cast of others, each of whom has a place on your marketing team:

Graphic designer: Remodelers can create wonderful designs for additions, kitchens, baths, or decks, but few clearly understand the essentials of graphic design. Find an experienced graphic designer who can add flair and professionalism to everything from your company logo to the job site postcard you'll be sending out. There are plenty of small, one- or two-person graphics companies that can affordably design and produce excellent marketing pieces.

To find a great graphic designer, ask your printer or other business associates for referrals or look on the bulletin board of office supply stores or copy centers (many designers post their business cards there). A lot of printers have expanded their services to include design, which gives you a one-stop shopping alternative.

Before you make any commitments to a graphic designer, interview the person and look through their portfolio of samples. Then interview several of their customers. Be sure that the designer you choose demonstrates a style that fits your company image.

Writer: Marketing writing is a specific skill that takes time to develop. Using a writer who is experienced in producing marketing text will provide you with a more effective piece, usually in less time. Your graphic designer usually will be able to recommend writers.

Printers: Printers, like remodelers, often specialize. Most companies need the services of two different types of printers—a quick printer for smaller, one- or two-color projects, and a second printer for large-quantity, more complex work. Sometimes you can find one company that can do both types of work and give you a competitive price.

While it's important to work with a company with which you feel comfortable, it's also important to find good value. At our company, we work with three different printers and usually ask all three for estimates on any given project. We've discovered that each company has certain types of work that they can do more efficiently and at a better price. We use all three printers throughout the course of a year.

Until you learn more about printing and can determine which printer is best for a particular job, we recommend asking for estimates from several printers for each project.

Mail house: Investing in the services of a mail house can be one of the most efficient ways to spend your marketing dollars if you're doing a number of larger mailings (1,000 pieces or more). A mail house can handle the labeling, stamping, and complicated sorting the Post Office requires to get the best rate. In addition, you can often use the mailing house's postal indicia (formatted information including a permit number) for bulk rate mailings or business reply mail—instead of investing in your own.

A mail house can take a database file containing all of your contacts and easily translate it into zip-code-sorted labels. It's usually inefficient to do this work in-house. Be sure to inform any mailing house that your mailing list is to be kept completely confidential. Ask your printer or your graphic designer for mail house recommendations.

Web site designer: As consumers increasingly use the Internet to locate quality companies, it's critical that your web site represents the image you've worked so hard to build. A web site designer should be able to guide you through the process of creating a user-friendly web site for your company. Because web design is a very easy business to enter, expertise and experience can vary greatly from one designer to another. Before you contract with any web designer, view web sites they have created to make sure their style fits your company's image and that the sites are **very easy to use!**

Here are some resources for finding marketing team members:

, The local chamber of commerce
, The local university (marketing, business, or graphic arts students make wonderfully economic employees, plus you get the benefit of fresh creativity)

- Your peers
- Neighbors and other business associates
- Your industry association.

Check around and interview several companies in each of the categories above until you find just the right fit for your company. A well-implemented marketing program—like a good remodeling job—is the result of careful planning that includes the owner's input, good follow-up by a company employee, and a team of subcontractors who deliver.

part two

DEVELOPING YOUR COMPANY'S PUBLIC FACE

Positioning Your Company:

What Is Your Image?

Carrying Image Throughout the Company

Image Marketing Plan and Budget

POSITIONING YOUR COMPANY: WHAT IS YOUR IMAGE?

Your target market develops an image of your company from a variety of sources—your jobs, signs, personnel, clientele, publicity, brochures, and other materials. What is the public's image of your company?

IMAGE: *a community's perception of something or someone.*

Every marketer works to control the quality of their image. It's crucial that all of the materials used to represent your company communicate a cohesive style that supports the niche you've chosen. A remodeler can claim that his or her company is professional, organized, and has design flair, but would the public describe the company that way if asked?

Because remodeling is an easy-entry industry with plenty of companies coming and going each year, one of the first things you must do is communicate to the market that your company is stable and will be around for a long time. Visually communicate that you're different—more professional, more reliable, more creative. You can do this with a professional array of company materials such as an attractive logo, stationery, sales and marketing tools, contracts, and more.

In addition to investing in materials that shout "We're professionals!" all of your materials should reflect expertise in your niche.

For example, design/build companies should have materials that demonstrate design flair; boring or ordinary materials won't cut it in that niche. Remodelers who work with banks should use marketing materials with a corporate feeling that fits into the bank environment—not something graphically avant-garde. Fit your materials to your target market—not to your personal taste. Also, remember what we said about choosing a graphic designer who can match your company image.

But before we begin to explore which materials to develop, let's look at two areas of marketing "homework." It's no use spreading your name and logo around if they aren't right. So let's start by reviewing these two essentials.

REMODELING YOUR COMPANY NAME

Many remodelers find they have names that don't communicate what they do in their business ("Smith Company," for example), or which could mislead ("Smith Construction" when they are actually design/build remodelers). This is a relatively easy problem to solve. "Smith" is the important part of this name and a change to "Smith Design and Remodeling," for instance, is a relatively small step. However, that change has some big benefits in marketing. Your signs and materials now clearly state what you do. Just seeing your company name attracts potential buyers; there's no explaining to do.

 S T R E E T SMARTS

Like many remodelers, Thomas Buckborough started his company by himself. The logical thing to do was to name the company after himself. Now, as a successful design/build company in Concord, Mass., he's happy with his choice.

"'Thomas E. Buckborough & Associates' communicates professionalism like the name of a lawyer's or doctor's office does," he says. "It tells our clients that there is a person standing behind this company. They feel comfortable that we'll deliver high-quality work since my name and reputation are on the line."

He supplements the company name with a tag line, "Fine Residential Designers and Remodelers," which communicates the specific services his firm offers.

■ ■ ■

When Dale Nikula created his Dennisport, Mass., remodeling company, he did what most remodelers do and incorporated his own name. The Dale R. Nikula Company, Inc., became very successful and its volume grew close to $6,000,000. That growth, and Dale's hard work to change the business from a "practice" in which the owner was integrally involved to a business organization, convinced him that it was time to take the next step and change the company's name.

In 2003, the company became Encore Construction Company, Inc. "I wanted to create more value for the company," Dale says. "I felt that moving it away from my name would make it more saleable—few people want to buy a company named after someone else—*and* would change the clients' expectations of my involvement. As Encore Construction, clients don't automatically expect to talk to me, the owner, about every job."

Plus, there's been an unexpected benefit. "I've found that my employees have a new sense of ownership now," he says. "They know that it's not just me running the company. It's helped them realize that future growth of the company and our profitability depends upon each person in the company."

■ ■ ■

DEVELOPING/UPDATING YOUR COMPANY LOGO

A logo is a graphic treatment of your company name. A logo may or may not include a graphic "symbol" as well. For example, IBM and Exxon use their names as their logos while Prudential Insurance incorporates the symbol of the "rock" and McDonald's has the Golden Arches™.

If you need a logo or if your logo needs to be updated, take the plunge and invest in the skills of a talented graphic designer to help you create a logo that has polish and flair.

Depending on the designer, the investment for a corporate package design can range from $1,000 to $3,500. Work with the designer until he or she comes up with a logo you'll want to use for the next 15 to 20 years. Since you'll be working hard to establish this logo in the marketplace, you won't want to change it in the near future.

STREETSMARTS

◀ 1

In 1961, George Gayler's father designed this logo, logo 1, using a script typeface that was popular at the time. This logo worked well for over 30 years.

In the early 1990's, George and his wife, Darlene, who co-owned the company with him at that time, decided the logo needed an upgrade. Since Gayler Construction Company had served the market for some time, they were reluctant to change the logo too much and possibly lose the recognition it had helped create for the company. So they contented themselves with a slight typeface update, as shown below, logo 2.

◀ 2

In the late 1990's, Darlene, who has a marketing background, took a hard look at the company logo and decided it was time for a redo. By this time, the company had moved to a more affluent area, now served a more upscale market, and had greatly increased its professionalism. Because the company served a relatively new market, the Gaylers weren't as worried about possibly losing recognition by overhauling the logo. It was time for a fresh start. "We wanted a logo that would communicate energy and innovation," Darlene says. "So I worked with a graphic designer to develop our new logo, which is up-to-date and lively."

The combination of black and soothing green represents the company's focus on environmentally friendly remodeling while the graphics symbolize rolling hills and structures. "This logo, with its unique shapes and colors, seems to be very recognizable as we regularly receive positive comments from our customers and friends," Darlene adds.

■ ■ ■

Here are some tips for creating a high-impact company logo:

› When considering the design, keep in mind how you'll use the logo. Using multiple colors and color screens might create a stunning logo, but reproducing such a colorful logo on all of your materials may be costly.

› The logo should be easy to read and simple in concept. Remember, you'll be using your logo on stationery, brochures, trucks, signs, and ads. Choose a logo that can be reproduced clearly in black and white.

› Don't be too gimmicky. Cartoon figures may work for selling inexpensive items, but remodeling buyers want stability and professionalism.

› There's a good chance your current logo can be updated to make it more polished and "now" without the expense of a complete redo.

DESIGN/BUILD

When Tom and Trish Schroeder founded their company in 1986, they felt it was important to have their ownership reflected. So they used the name TJ Schroeder Construction, Inc., for their Fairfax, Va., company.

"It was after one of our clients told us that our name didn't reflect what we do that we thought we'd change the name and upgrade the logo," says Trish. Since the design/build process they practiced became more sophisticated and was better accepted by consumers, the Schroeders decided to incorporate that term into their company's new name.

In 2001, they changed the name to Schroeder Design/Build, and began to develop a logo. Trish says, "We wanted to move away from the mom-and-pop image. We wanted a logo that was sleek and professional." So they turned to designer Cristina Diez de Medina, president of A Scribbler's Press in Kensington, Md., for help.

After many renditions flew back and forth between the designer and the remodelers, they settled on a logo featuring a stylish typeface and a triangle symbol that is reproduced in shiny silver on all of Schroeder Design/Build's marketing materials.

"We wanted something out of the ordinary, something to set us aside from the other guys," Trish says, "so we went the extra step with the silver metallic symbol. It costs us more every step of the way—from the additional cost of foil for printing to the specially ordered embroidery thread for our company shirts. But it is all worth it to have a logo that is just a little bit more special than anyone one else's."

▲

PUTTING YOUR IMAGE ON PAPER

After you've developed your company name and logo, your printer can convert them into a stationery package. Depending on your budget and needs, your package will include at least some of the following:

‣ Stationery
‣ Second sheets
‣ Note cards and envelopes
‣ Fax sheets
‣ Letter size envelopes
‣ Large envelopes
‣ Labels
‣ Business cards
‣ Presentation folders

Many companies slowly use up the materials they already have on hand and then transition into their "new" look piece by piece. Be sure your graphic designer provides you with a digital version of your logo so that you can easily use it on company documents, e-mails, and on your web site.

LEAVE-BEHIND PACKETS

Many companies want to provide their prospective clients with information to help them make an informed decision. So, after the first meeting, they may leave a packet of materials for the prospect's review. These packets often include testimonial letters from clients, article reprints, details on the company's services, and more.

Craig Deimler, ▶
vice president of
Deimler & Sons
Construction, Inc.,
Harrisburg, Pa.,
worked with a
designer to
created this
sleek presentation
folder featuring
the company logo.

When presenting materials to your clients, use an attractive folder to support your highly professional image. Custom folders can be created specifically for your company or you can purchase high-end folders at an office supply store and customize them with company labels.

Be sure that the materials in the folder look fresh and clean. Copies of materials are acceptable but should be crisp and easily readable. If your original newspaper article, for example, is getting beat up, ask a graphic designer to rework it to give you a fresh original.

DEVELOPING A COMPANY BROCHURE

A professionally designed brochure enhances an established company's ability to sell its services at a higher price. It's part of the packaging. Brochures can be left behind for prospects after sales meetings, direct mailed before the initial meeting, handed out at home shows, and can be used for many other purposes.

Like every marketing piece you'll develop for your company, you can have the Chevy or the Mercedes version. Your choice depends on two criteria:

1. Your budget.

2. The way you want your clients to perceive your company.

Your brochure budget will depend on:
) The size of the brochure
) The paper you choose
) Whether the brochure will be full color or black and white
) Whether or not you will include photos
) The cost of the designer, writer, and printer
) How well organized you are at the beginning. Just like change orders can disrupt a project's schedule and increase its cost, last-minute changes will increase the cost of your brochure.
) A number of other factors.

The second criteria, the way you want clients to perceive your company—is equally important. Think of it this way: Each marketing tactic you develop acts as a mini-radio transmitter sending a message. The material's words and look communicate the message. If you serve an upper class or wealthy clientele, avoid materials that look too loud or inexpensive. If your market is people with modest incomes, some clients could be put off by materials that look too rich.

Here are some guidelines to help you develop your brochure:

1. Most brochures are good for only two to three years. Don't worry about developing the perfect piece; just get it done. However, make sure all the text is correctly spelled and is grammatically correct.

2. If you need a starter brochure, consider using one of the generic brochures industry associations develop. Add a company label to customize it. The good news: It's ready to use, it's been professionally developed, and it's inexpensive. The bad news: It isn't really about you.

3. How will you get the brochure to prospects? Using a self-mailer format makes it easy to use as a direct mail piece. If you're planning to send the brochure to large groups of people, print it with the bulk-mail indicia in place. When sending just a few, place the first-class stamp over the indicia and mail. This gives you maximum flexibility.

4. If you may occasionally mail the brochure in an envelope, size it to fit in a standard envelope.

5. Make sure the look matches your company materials' color(s), typeface, an ' logo.

6. Creating the copy is probably the most difficult task you'll do. Use headlines and subheads to clarify your major benefit messages. Understanding your niche and your main benefits will help you communicate with your clients. Professional writing help is worth every penny you may invest in it.

7. Be sure to leave plenty of white space—unused areas—to make the brochure easy to read.

CARRYING IMAGE THROUGHOUT THE COMPANY

Once you've created a dynamite logo for your company, use it consistently throughout all of your marketing efforts. The same colors, the same typefaces, and the same configuration should be used on your stationery, presentation packet, brochure, company trucks, uniforms, advertisements, job site signs, contracts, change orders, and anything else you use to communicate with your customers and prospects.

COMPANY TRUCKS: YOUR TRAVELING BILLBOARDS

Your company trucks act as moving billboards for your company. Using your company logo and color(s) on your trucks greatly increases market awareness. Many remodelers who have spent the money to add signage to their vehicles say that it's one of their most effective lead generation tools. In addition, prospects coming to the company from other sources who learn about the company in other ways often see and recognize the company trucks, giving the company a head start on the sale.

Stay away from the small, old-fashioned, magnetic signs that remodeling industry newcomers use. You're a pro. You charge more, and you must demonstrate your creativity and class in every area of your business. Do it right, or don't do it at all.

But beware, once your trucks have signs, that identification can be used for or against you. Drivers of these moving billboards must park legally, off the grass, and use the highest levels of driving courtesy on the road. Exhibiting road rage or other improper use of this marketing tool can cause far-reaching, negative ripples that may injure your company image.

⬦ STREET SMARTS

Company vans at Benvenuti & Stein, Inc., in Evanston, Ill., are more than a means of getting to and from work. They're company billboards on wheels. Each van features Benvenuti & Stein's logo and contact information and they're getting a lot of attention around town.

"I've gotten a lot of responses from people who say, 'You obviously do a lot of work in our area; therefore you must be okay,' " says Geno Benvenuti, company president. "Very often, that closes the deal before we even meet them."

In lieu of a two-dollar-an-hour raise, Benvenuti gives his carpenters a company van and pays for insurance and repairs. The money he saves on raises coupled with the amount he is able to write off covers the cost of the 10 vans he now has on the road.

"Our vans have created a real sense of establishment in our area. They build brand identity and create name recognition," Benvenuti says. "In many of the suburbs in which we work, we're not allowed to post job signs to advertise, so having the vans parked at the job site gets our message out."

■ ■ ■

If possible, all of your vehicles should be the same color—preferably one that's consistent with the company colors. Signage should include a large, easily identified logo, your phone number, web site, and a list of services. Trucks should always be well maintained, neat, and clean to leave a good impression.

Scientific studies on the effectiveness of truck signs have been published. The American Trucking Association and 3M counted the people who saw one truck with signage driving in an urban area for 4 1/2 hours a day, five days a week. In one year, that truck was seen and noted by 5 million people. With that kind of exposure, spending $800 to $2,000 on a top-quality paint job or decaling would be a bargain! But again, don't do an ordinary job—do an extraordinary job.

▼

TRUCK SIGNAGE

Signage technology has come a long way! Now you can wrap your vehicles and trailers in beautiful, full-color photography with digital signange. What a compelling way to demonstrate your expertise! Just think how eye-catching your vehicle would be with a photo of that beautiful portico or room addition on the side.

Of course, traditional options are still available as well. Many businesses choose to restrict their signage to their logo and perhaps a tag line. The truck signage you choose depends on your budget and available photography resources. Signs that are produced digitally as well as those using traditional methods are printed on vinyl and applied with adhesive backing.

▲ *Patti McDaniel, president of Boardwalk Builders, Inc., has created a dynamic moving billboard with her job trailers.*

Digital Signage

Investment per truck: $900 to $1,000

Pros

Many colors available

Perfect for clear, crisp photography

Cons

Can cost up to four times more than traditional truck signage

Lasts only two to four years

Traditional Truck Signage

Investment per truck: $300 to $400

Pros

Less expensive

More durable; lasts four to six years

Cons

Limited colors

Not applicable for reproducing photography

Search the Internet for truck signage.

▲

PROFESSIONALIZE YOUR STAFF WITH UNIFORMS

Company uniforms are one of the easiest ways to differentiate your business from your competitors. Uniforms can also enhance the team-spirit atmosphere by creating a company "look" that everyone embraces.

A company uniform can be as informal as a polo-style shirt imprinted with the company logo and worn with blue jeans or shorts, or as formal as pants worn with a matching shirt embroidered with a carpenter's or crew member's name.

Your goal is to create name awareness while maintaining a consistently professional appearance for everyone who represents your company. There are several ways to handle a uniform program:

▸ Purchase and provide a certain number of uniforms at the beginning of the program for all employees. Providing five or six uniforms is common, although some remodelers have provided up to 12 polo shirts for each of their carpenters. As the initial supply is depleted, employees are allowed to purchase additional uniform components at half price and the company picks up the other half of the cost. Employees are responsible for laundering their own uniforms.

▸ Rent uniforms from a uniform supply company. The company will drop off clean uniforms once a week when it picks up dirty ones to launder. This way, everyone has a clean supply on hand. Personalization may cost extra.

▸ Some companies provide jackets, sweatshirts, or stocking hats in colder weather.

Some remodelers say that crews complain about uniforms being uncomfortable, but with today's breathable fabrics, that complaint is unfounded. After all, how can anyone complain about a polo shirt being uncomfortable?

To introduce the program, explain to your staff how uniforms will favorably support your company's image in the market place. Then, ask them to vote on a couple of affordable uniform alternatives. The benefits you gain through increased recognition and enhanced public image will far outweigh the investment you will have to make on buying or renting uniforms.

COMPANY SIGNS SEND A MESSAGE

One of the most effective marketing tools you'll ever use is company signs. If your company is located in a building that allows company signage, you have a powerful marketing tool at your disposal—take advantage of it! Whether you are located on a busy retail street or an industrial park, your signage should be easily readable and consistent with the rest of your company's materials. Your logo should be large enough to see and recognize. If your logo doesn't indicate your niche clearly enough, include a tagline statement of your services (for example, "The Best in High Quality Residential Remodeling").

YOUR OFFICE PROVIDES CLUES

Construction offices often contain messy boxes of old blueprints, Sweet's catalogs from the mid '90s, boxed and unboxed job site materials, an old transit leaning against the wall, and desks that the local bank threw out (plus an occasional flush door used as a desk). This works fine for a time, but once your office is open to the public, especially to potential clients, the rules change!

Don't worry; the change is worth it. Remodelers who have opened their offices as meeting places for prospects, customers, suppliers, and subs are convinced that using their offices as selling tools is very powerful. We recommend you meet your prospects for the second meeting in your office, but be sure that it reflects the company's image that you have established. A wonderful company packet, the best sales presentation, and a beautifully organized proposal can all be undermined by a sloppy, dirty, office environment.

Support your claims of high-quality work by hanging framed, complimentary letters from clients, articles from magazines, feature newspaper articles, and association membership certificates on the walls. Professional photos of beautiful jobs (before and after shots, if possible) should be enlarged and hung. Keep samples and files neatly stored until needed. Floors and counter surfaces should sparkle. And remember the bathroom! Your prospects will judge you by the way you maintain that space, too!

Many remodelers who don't have showrooms build a variety of details into their offices that can be used as examples for their clients. For instance, you can install recessed, fluorescent, and incandescent lighting. Countertops can be made of laminate, solid surfacing, granite, and stainless steel. The cabinet lines you sell can be used for built-in bookshelves, desks, or kitchenettes. Windows can be used in interior walls.

Now your office is not only great looking but acts as a mini-showroom to showcase samples of the materials you use. Prospects will notice that you've created a high-quality environment for yourself and will feel more comfortable about your ability to keep their home neat and clean while you're working there.

▲ Jonas Carnemark and his team are well known for their creative remodeling projects. With an open floorplan, avant-garde furnishings, and bright colors, their office supports this image. Anyone entering the office knows instantly that CARNEMARK systems + design inc, Bethesda, Md., is an artistic, innovative company.

PERFORMING WELL IS THE BEST IMAGE

Great-looking trucks, beautiful stationery, and a smashing office can never make up for doing poor work on the job. All your marketing must be supported by the ability to do technically masterful work and to do it quickly and neatly and with happy clients at the end. To make sure that the wonderful perception of your company isn't tainted by inconsiderate behavior, most remodelers ask their employees to follow job rules such as no smoking, no radios, no debris accumulation, and no tools left on site.

Remember, marketing is 90% doing things very well and 10% letting others know about it.

IMAGE MARKETING PLAN AND BUDGET

Consider the image-enhancing tools you currently use and how you will update your image throughout the company. Below, you'll find a wish list that you'll add to a number of times as you work your way through the book. If budget becomes an issue, only implement the greatest priority materials. At this point, just use ballpark expenses to begin building your overall marketing budget.

TACTICS/EFFORTS COST

Company logo $ ———————————

Collateral materials $ ———————————
(stationery, brochures, etc.)

Truck signage $ ———————————

Uniforms $ ———————————

Company signage $ ———————————

Office $ ———————————

Other $ ———————————

TOTAL BUDGET $ ———————————

part three

INCREASING REPEAT BUSINESS AND REFERRAL LEADS

Focusing on Your Best Sources of Business

Creating Loyalty With Regular Mailings

Saying "Thanks" With Customer Gifts

Creating a Referral Program

Business Contacts Deliver Business

Testimonials Pack a Wallop

Circle of Influence Marketing Plan and Budget

FOCUSING ON YOUR BEST SOURCES OF BUSINESS

The two most desired business sources for every remodeler are:

▸ Repeat business from an existing client

▸ A referral to a prospective customer from an existing client or friend of the company

Many companies find that 75% or more of their business comes from these two sources alone—and they represent pure gold if properly mined. Unfortunately, many remodelers look for gold everywhere but in their own back yard. A myth that exists in the remodeling world says that repeat business and referral leads will come to you without your lifting a finger. Too many remodelers believe this myth and spend all their effort and money trying to look outside of this valuable community for business. The sad thing is that these outside sources typically deliver leads that are more expensive and of lesser quality.

We want to share a critical, proven principle of marketing:

The Golden Rule of Marketing
You can double the repeat business and number of referral leads you receive if you constantly market back to your Circle of Influence.

CAPTURING BUSINESS FROM REPEAT CUSTOMERS

Securing customers is one of the toughest parts of this business. Once you've sold someone a project, do everything you can to capture all of the remodeling work that they'll purchase in the years to come. We all know that it costs much more to find and sell a new customer than it does to re-sell an existing customer, so focus your efforts on your previous customers first.

Communication is the key to obtaining the maximum amount of repeat business. Continually stay in touch with your clients to maintain what advertising agency folks call "top of mind awareness" (TOMA). Your marketing goal is to have your previous clients consider your company first when beginning a remodeling project. If you don't stay in touch with them to remind them about the quality service you delivered, they simply won't remember!

Picture this: You're in the grocery store and run into clients for whom you completed a successful kitchen remodel several years ago. In the course of a friendly, warm conversation, the clients mention that they just finished an extensive addition to their home! You're dismayed and quickly ask, "Why didn't you call us?" The typical answer is, "We didn't know you did that kind of work." Your heart sinks as you realize that your marketing program could have easily changed this scenario.

Just as you need to remind your customers about the service and quality product you once provided them, you also must frequently talk about the array of services you bring to the table. Never assume that your previous clients know everything that you offer. It's your job to educate them.

THE IMPORTANCE OF REFERRAL LEADS

According to the National Association of the Remodeling Industry (NARI), nearly 50% of all incoming jobs to contractors come from client referrals. You may find the percentage to be far greater in your own company. A national survey by *Remodeling* magazine supports the notion that a majority of remodeling business comes from personal referrals. In the survey, homeowners were asked to list the sources that they used to find a contractor. Some 70% counted on either direct remodeling experience or their friends and relatives to help them find a contractor.

Because this source of business is so important to your company, make it a top priority to create a program that encourages referrals.

Referrals are win-win. They assure the homeowner that the remodeler they are contacting is professional and delivers what had been promised. For remodelers, referrals deliver a prospect who typically values more than just price and is much more likely to buy than the random lead from the phone book or a newspaper ad.

There's no argument that the highest quality lead is a referral. Remodelers have found that:

▸ The close ratio on these leads far surpasses that of any other source.

▸ The cost of a referral lead is the least expensive of any.

▸ The referrer often gives the prospect a lot of information about the company, which sets the tone for the remodeler to make the sale.

By speaking to their friend or neighbor about their project, a prospect probably knows:

▸ You're not the cheapest remodeler in town, but you offer good value.

▸ You deliver what you promise.

▸ Your personnel are pleasant, friendly, and courteous craftspeople.

▸ You keep the job site clean and neat.

▸ You have worked for others who are similar to the prospect, and those other customers are happy with your work.

Remember, referrals come from a larger group of people than just your previous customers. Friends, social acquaintances, and business associates also can send referrals your way. We call this extended group your Circle of Influence. This includes not only previous customers, but also business associates like suppliers, your insurance agent, and the director of your local association as well as personal contacts like the PTA president and the parents you've met through your child's Little League. Stop now and create a list of these influential people. Then create a program that will help these people think of your company when they're presented with an opportunity to refer you.

What's the key to encouraging referrals from this wonderful group? Communication! Let's talk about the details.

DEVELOPING A DATABASE

Use a computerized database to keep track of your clients, friends of the company, and their various contact information. The database should include basic information such as address, home and work phone numbers, e-mail address, type of project, and lead source. It can also include optional items like map coordinates, profession, family size, ages of clients, family members living at home, and more.

We recommend that you maintain information about customers for at least five years after you finish a project for them. This provides you with a wonderful list of people who know your company, appreciate the services you offer, and could refer dozens of new prospects your way.

There are many software programs that make contact management easy. In our offices we use *ACT! (www.act.com)*. It's easy to use and has an add-on product called *Better ACT!* produced by 9 Dots, Inc. that provides remodelers with job tracking information as well as common templates, letters, and other tools. Visit our web site *(www.RemodelersAdvantage.com)* for more information. Other popular software programs include *Goldmine (www.frontrange.com)*, and Intuit's new *Quick-Books Customer Manager (www.intuit.com)*.

Some remodelers use *Outlook (www.microsoft.com/office/ outlook)* to help them manage their customer lists. This computer program and those mentioned above make it simple to manage your customer database in-house.

CREATING A COMMUNICATIONS PROGRAM

Once you've developed your Circle of Influence list, stay in touch with these people at least four times a year. Some remodelers who know the importance of this referral base contact their clients up to seven times each year! While the message is soft (no hard selling here), your goal is two-fold: To encourage referrals and to capture future business from this valuable group.

How you contact this group isn't as important as the fact that your company name is in front of their eyes on a regular basis. Here are some ways you can stay in touch:

- Newsletters
- Informative letters on your letterhead
- Holiday cards
- Invitations to a home show
- Delivering a gift after the project is finished
- Telephone calls on the anniversary of their project completion
- Notices of new services offered
- Updates on referral programs
- Announcements of special events, such as
  - Television or magazine coverage
  - Open houses
  - Your company's anniversary

Think creatively! There are many ways you can stay in touch.

BE SURE TO SAY "THANKS" FOR THE GOLDEN REFERRAL

When you receive a referral, say thanks immediately! A note or phone call to thank the person who sent the lead will be noticed and appreciated. Some remodelers enclose a gift certificate (perhaps a $10 certificate to the local bookstore you remodeled—make both clients happy—or a certificate to a gourmet bakery) or a lottery ticket ("Thanks a million!") as a special thanks. You probably know people who refer business to you again and again and again. They're very special supporters of your company. Say thanks by taking them to lunch, to the ballpark, or to a play. They need to know that you value their support.

CREATING LOYALTY WITH REGULAR MAILINGS

A mail campaign is one of the easiest ways to keep in touch with your clients. Here are some ideas on what you could send:

NEWSLETTERS ARE DYNAMITE TOOLS

Newsletters are excellent tools for staying in touch with your Circle of Influence. Attractive, lively newsletters can communicate valuable information in an interesting, easy-to-read format. They communicate your company's expertise and personality. Costs for a newsletter can be minimal if you produce it yourself, but can amount to thousands of dollars a year for a professionally produced, full-color version.

Here are some tips for creating a high-impact, user-friendly newsletter:

▶ Keep the stories short and easy to read. People are too busy to read long stories.

- Two sides of an 8 ½" x 11" sheet is all you really need. While you can create a multi-page "magazine," we recommend staying with four pages or fewer.

- Keep it soft-sell if you want it to be read. Don't use a newsletter as a vehicle for a hard-sell promotion. Remember, you're selling to the already converted.

- Include stories about your company such as awards won, certificates earned, personnel profiles, special charity projects you're involved in, etc.

- Throw story ideas into a file. Then simply pull them out when it's time for the newsletter. You'll find you have plenty of material.

- Trade magazines (those written for a particular industry or type of business) will often let you reprint a survey, a study, or a funny column if you ask permission.

- List current jobs, such as: "Mary and Tim Johnson, Main Street, Hustonville Township." Neighbors are always interested and it reinforces your credibility.

- If you want color in the masthead (the part of the newsletter with the company's and newsletter's names, issue date, etc.), but you don't want to pay for color each time you print, have a year's supply of newsletter "templates" printed in color. Then you can copy or print your text in black ink onto the template.

- If your budget is small, write a two-page (front and back of one sheet) newsletter on your company letterhead.

- Check out the newsletter services that provide semi-customized newsletters. Using one of these services may cut your costs considerably. Watch the classified ads in the back of trade magazines or look for the services' booths at trade shows. *Remodeling Tips* is one popular newsletter service. Find details at *www.RTIncorporated.com*.

STREET SMARTS

Following are two different newsletters with two very different looks. Each is full-color and includes gorgeous photography of a featured project. Each newsletter includes articles of interest to homeowners throughout the area.

▼ *Winans Construction, Inc., Oakland, Calif.*

WINANS
Beautiful Work with Care Since 1978

Remodel Right

SPRING 2003   Remodeling News from Winans Construction, Inc.

Unique Remodeling Solution:
A Backyard Cottage Gives A Family Member Autonomy

Q : Tell us about this project. A: My mother was in the early stages of Alzheimer's and was living alone. We knew she needed our care, but she also preferred to have her own space. Her old house was close to noise and traffic and was two stories so it was difficult for her to get around in. After much research, we decided to build a separate cottage in our backyard for her to live in. Q: What did you do with the space? A: This cute little house has a bedroom, bathroom, and a fully-equipped galley kitchen. It's one story which is so much easier for my mother. It's enough for anyone to live comfortably and still have privacy. Q: How about the style of the building and the rooms? A: The outside is very modern and angular, which is exactly what we wanted. Anne Phillips, our architect, suggested adding a trellis, and plants and

flowers have already begun to grow beautifully up to reach it. There's also a lovely patio in front that gets lots of sun most of the day. Q: What about the inside? A: We wanted a Japanese style, so we chose a light, modern and open design with a cathedral ceiling and several wonderful arched windows. The floors are concrete throughout. And there are two sets of beautiful French doors that open onto the patio– one set that opens out from the kitchen, and one from the bedroom. Q: How did you like working with Winans? A: I was very impressed that they took the time to fully understand our needs and to address them in making this space work for my family. They gave lots of valuable input throughout the process and paid attention to detail at every turn. We are very satisfied with the result!

This cottage for an aging parent has a bedroom, bathroom, and fully-equipped galley kitchen along with a patio in front.

The cathedral ceiling adds to the light and airy environment of the bedroom.

3947 Opal Street, Oakland, California 94609 510.653.7288 e: info@winconinc.com www.winconinc.com

"ON THE HOUSE"

The month of May brought more than spring flowers. It brought over 100 people to Blackdog's showroom for an Open House and day of free home remodeling seminars. Joining us was special guest Michael Payne, host and interior designer for HGTV's *"Designing for the Sexes."* His seminar, *The Most Common Design Dilemmas Between Couples*, brought forth an abundance of laughter, nods and knowing smiles among the dozens of partners in attendance as well as a host of practical tips and sound advice.

But there was much more. Homeowners also walked away with a better understanding of *What You Need to Know When Remodeling Your Home, Space Planning on A Budget: Frugal Design & Fabulous Results!* and *Building Equity into Your Remodeling Project with Windows & Doors.*

In light of a wonderful turn-out and a desire to provide education to homeowners, Blackdog is pleased to announce that another series of free home remodeling seminars will be offered next spring at our showroom, where we will be joined once again by the distinguished Michael Payne.

It didn't take long for Michael Payne to captivate the audience with true tales of spousal stand-offs.

▲ **Blackdog Builders, Inc. Salem, N.H.**

■ ■ ■

To help make newsletter writing easier, we've included twelve ready-to-use articles in Part Eight. Just choose what you like and use it in your next newsletter.

LETTERS TO PRODUCE LEADS

Some of the most sophisticated remodelers send simple letters on their company letterhead two or three times a year. Sometimes they alternate letters, newsletters, and invitations to open houses or home shows.

These letters can provide information about a new product or a new system your company has implemented, or inform readers about a new development in the remodeling industry.

Whatever you write, focus on the benefits to the reader. For example, your letter might include a statement about a new estimating system you've implemented. That's nice, but your clients don't really care until you tell them about the benefits: "This means we'll be able to produce accurate estimates much more quickly to give you the detailed information you need to make intelligent decisions." In all your marketing efforts, focus on what's in it for your prospects and customers.

Here are three ready-to-use letters written for Thanksgiving, Valentine's Day, and late winter. You can send them as-is to your clients (after you add your name and company name, of course), or use them as templates to start writing letters for any occasion.

THANKSGIVING LETTER SAMPLE

Dear Friends of (your company name),

Especially at this time of year, we realize that we have a great deal to be thankful for. One of our greatest blessings is the group of wonderful customers we've had the pleasure to work for over the past few years.

We rely on friends like you for our success. Thank you for the business you've entrusted to us and for the referrals you've sent our way. You've made us what we are today!

> Cordially,
> (Your Name)
> (Company Name)

P.S. Call us today to get started on your project!

VALENTINE'S DAY LETTER SAMPLE

(Use "Love" stamps from the Post Office)

Dear Friends of (your company name),

It's Valentine's Day, so there's no better time to say "We love our customers!" We love helping you improve your home. We love working with you to find just the right solution. And we love seeing your smiling face when the project is done. That's what keeps us going. So thank you again for the business and referrals you've sent our way and please call us if you'd like to talk about your upcoming home improvement plans. We'd love to hear from you!

> Cordially,
> (Your Name)
> (Company Name)

P.S. With low interest rates, there has never been a better time to remodel.

LATE WINTER LETTER SAMPLE

Dear Friends of (your company name),

Soon spring will be springing and we'll all want our homes to be in top condition. To beat the rush and avoid delays, let's begin planning your remodeling or renovation projects now.

Whether you're considering a new kitchen, a basement renovation, or a new addition, the best remodeling projects are carefully planned to give you the best solution to your space needs. That's where we come in. For years, we've been working with homeowners like you to create beautiful homes that make living a pleasure and a convenience—a home that will make you proud. So call us today to schedule an appointment to discuss your remodeling or renovation plans. With an early start, your home could be blooming right along with the flowers!

> Cordially,
> (Your Name)
> (Company Name)

P.S. As you're looking through magazines or newspapers, clip your favorite room photos for an "idea file" to keep track of the styles and colors you like best. Then let us show you how to incorporate those ideas into your home.

▲

STREET SMARTS

When the team at Silver Bullet Design & Build, Inc., in Minneapolis, Minn., celebrated the company's 25th year in business, they wanted to let their customers know about this important milestone. "We know that homeowners look for companies with longevity," says president Terry Streich. "Companies that have been in business for some time demonstrate stability and quality."

The amusing headline plays off the company name and lets customers know that Terry and his employees don't take themselves too seriously!

■ ■ ■

ANNOUNCEMENTS OF SPECIAL EVENTS

Every company has special events that take place from time to time. These events might include the company's anniversary, winning a special award, hiring a new key employee, being featured in a newspaper or magazine story, or a variety of other things. Let your Circle of Influence know about special events with special mailings.

▼

Lee Kimball Kitchens, Inc., Boston, Mass., had a project that was going to be featured on Home and Garden TV (HGTV). Because it wasn't an every-day event, the company wanted to let everyone know about it. The owners created a beautiful, full-color postcard alerting the readers about the upcoming program. Whether or not the clients watched the HGTV segment, they received some important information—Lee Kimball Kitchens produces projects good enough for television! Wow!

USING HOLIDAY CARDS CREATIVELY

Staying in touch with your clients on a regular basis requires some creativity. Hundreds of remodelers use holiday greeting cards for this purpose. It's easy to use pre-printed, attractive cards, but make sure that your message doesn't get lost in the pack.

The most popular time for sending out holiday cards is during the December holiday season. While it's better than nothing, you're sacrificing your impact by following the crowd. Think about all of the cards you receive during this season—probably dozens from all your vendors as well as friends and family.

But how many cards do you receive to celebrate St. Patrick's Day, Groundhog Day, St. Valentine's Day, or Halloween? A card sent out for these or other offbeat holidays can stand out dramatically!

Here are some ideas for customized cards you can create:

▸ For Halloween, "Remodeling is a tricky business but working with you is a real treat."

▸ For St. Valentine's Day, "We love our customers. Thank you for helping to make us such a success!"

▸ For St. Patrick's Day, "Faith and Begorrah! Happy St. Patrick's Day to all our friends. The luck of the Irish was upon us when you chose us as your remodeling company. Thanks!"

Be creative, be clever, and be different if you want people to notice and remember your greeting card and your company. Don't follow the crowd. Talk to your graphic artist about designing a clever, stand-out card for your company.

PROJECT PROFILES

Clients love to see other people's projects. If you're working on a particularly nice project, use that as an excuse for a mailing. Let your clients know what kind of work you're currently doing. This works particularly well if you are trying to become known for a slightly different kind of project than you typically produce. For example, if you want to target a larger job size or a particular type of project, feature those kinds of jobs in your marketing materials.

Beautiful professional photography on an 8 ½" x 11" sheet or a postcard is an eye-catching way to show off your work.

▲ *This beautiful project profile sheet was developed by ADR Builders, Ltd., Timonium, Md.*

SAYING "THANKS" WITH CUSTOMER GIFTS

Many remodelers keep their customers feeling good about their companies by presenting them with tokens of appreciation when their projects are completed. A gift lets your customers know that you value the business they've given to your company.

The gift doesn't have to be large or expensive, but should reflect a sincere show of thanks. When purchasing a gift, be sure to buy something that will be around the home for a considerable time. Wine, cheese, candy, and flowers are poor gifts because they disappear shortly after the customer receives them.

Some great gift ideas include:

▸ A nicely organized binder full of the customers' project information such as the warranties, paint color reference numbers, pertinent telephone numbers, etc. Add a "before" and "after" photo to top it off.

▸ An attractively framed, professional photo of the finished project. Not only will the customer appreciate the effort you took, the neighbors will see it when it's hung on the wall. When the neighbors exclaim with delight, the customer will be only too happy to mention your company name!

▸ A magazine subscription will remind your customer of your great service all year long. Tip: When filling out the subscription card, have the magazine sent to your customer at their address, but write in your company's name as the recipient. This way, the customer will see your company name each and every month.

▸ A matted and framed pen-and-ink sketch of the home.

▸ Something that relates to the customer's personal interest or a hobby.

- A coordinating silk or dried-flower arrangement.

- An attractive brass or ceramic planter with a healthy house plant.

- A fruit or ornamental tree for the yard. Ask the clients first if they'd like this and ask where they want it planted.

A gift at the end of each job subtly steers the client into your Circle of Influence and creates a special feeling of goodwill.

CREATING A REFERRAL PROGRAM

A referral program is a system that encourages your previous clients and other Circle of Influence contacts to send their friends or associates who are considering remodeling to your company. Here are some referral-program strategies remodelers around the country have used successfully:

- At the bottom of the evaluation form you send when a project is completed, ask your customers to fill in the name and mailing address of anyone they know who is considering remodeling. For example: "Are any of your friends or neighbors thinking of remodeling? Please let us know and we'll be happy to provide them with important information to help plan their remodeling project."

- Provide a small gift—such as a $50–$100 gift certificate for dinner for two at a local restaurant—to anyone who provides a lead that turns into a project.

- Create a coupon that your customer gives to a prospect, and that the prospect then returns to you. This coupon represents a free small offering to the prospect when they sign up, and a gift to the customer who referred the prospect to you.

- A number of remodelers hold special events for their Circle of Influence members. This might be a summer picnic or a winter bash, with food, drink, and fun.

- Whenever your company participates in a marketing activity, consider how you can involve your Circle of Influence friends in a special way. Going to be in a home show? Offer them two free tickets. Holding an open house? Be sure they're invited.

Remember, sowing relationships and harvesting leads from your Circle of Influence is your number-one marketing effort. By using this strategy, you will reap the most important, easiest-to-sell leads. Don't skimp here!

The key to a successful referral program is to remind people that the program exists! If your company has entered a contest, keep them up-to-date on its progress, or include in your newsletter a list of folks who have taken advantage of your referral program. The more people hear about it, the more likely they are to participate.

▼

David and Karen Merrill, owners of Merrill Contracting & Remodeling, Inc., in Arlington, Va., host a large neighborhood party each year. They invite dozens of their clients and families to the event, which includes a catered barbecue meal, snow cones, a moon bounce, and face painting for the kids, plus live music and socializing for the adults.

Because the Merrills work within a small geographic area, many of their clients know one another. Once the invitations are sent out, the neighborhood begins to buzz with anticipation. It's become such a popular event that even non-clients ask for invitations! In recent years, more than 250 people have attended the party. The Merrills typically invest between $5,000 and $8,000 to host it. "So much of our business is community-based that we know this event has an impact," David says. "It's just one more time that people think of our company."

▲

STREET SMARTS

Alure Home Improvements in Hicksville, N.Y., knows that much of its growth as a $25,000,000 company is due to the hundreds of referrals it receives each year. But the referrals don't just fall into its lap! The Alure staff has created a wonderful program to entice their previous clients to send hundreds of thousands of dollars in business to the company.

The program is called Partner Points. Clients can earn points in two ways: When they hire Alure to do a project on their home, they earn Partner Points equal to the contract price of their project. They also earn points by referring friends, family, and co-workers. The previous client and the new client each earn points equal to the contract price of the new client's project.

Clients who accumulate 200,000 points receive an all-inclusive vacation for two! The program is promoted throughout the year in Alure's newsletter and on its web site, as well as through special showroom parties held every month. In 2002, Alure sent five couples on vacation trips. The result? Alure gets hundreds of leads each year from the Partner Points program. President Sal Ferro says, "Referral leads are easier to sell and they are focused on value, not price. Now we have our clients selling for us!"

■ ■ ■

BUSINESS CONTACTS DELIVER BUSINESS

Referrals from clients are wonderful, but don't overlook the referrals that can result from your business relationships. Create a referral program for your business allies to encourage them to bring business your way. The most effective method of encouraging referral leads from your business associates is by maintaining a healthy personal relationship with all of your contacts. Make it a policy to take a contact out to lunch at least once a month. Keep those relationships alive and thriving.

Remember that referrals work both ways. If you have the opportunity, be sure to refer prospects to the companies that are helping you out. As they begin to see business flowing their way, they'll be more inclined to think of your company when they encounter people who are considering remodeling.

Some remodelers join local business networking groups made up of non-competing companies that meet regularly to give each other leads. Others stay active in their local Chambers of Commerce. Many remodelers have found their time well spent when they participate with local businesses in a community-based club (Kiwanis or Rotary International Clubs, for example).

While all types of business people can refer prospects, here are some professionals that remodelers particularly rely on:

Real estate agents. Most people remodel their homes within two years of purchasing them. Some make plans to remodel before they purchase. By helping the prospective buyer think through the remodeling possibilities, you're also helping the real estate agent close the sale. It can be a win-win situation.

This relationship may present pitfalls you can avoid by clearly communicating with the agent. For example, some agents may misuse your services and call you out to talk to prospective home buyers who are have not committed to a home. Then, when they hear about the costs to remodel it, the prospects drop the idea and you've wasted your time. And, if would-be buyers decide not to purchase a house when they learn how much they need to spend on remodeling, your time has been wasted and you may have an agent who blames you for losing the sale. It's important that you clarify your services and prices to the agent up-front.

Some remodelers who receive referrals from real estate agents avoid wasting time by asking the homeowner to pay them a small consultation fee before they work together. This eliminates people who aren't serious about the project.

Subcontractors. Electricians, plumbers, drywall specialists, and other subcontractors come in contact with dozens of prospects that may have business for you. Homeowners consider a subcontractor's recommendation highly credible.

Architects. Many remodelers have alliances with architects. When the remodeler can't handle the design needs of a client, he or she will bring in an architect to help. This helps your company by giving you the ability to offer additional services to the client and helps the architect by bringing in business.

A key point: Maintain control over the prospect at all times. Handing over the lead to the architect gives him or her free rein to bring in other contractors to bid on jobs. See *Mastering the Business of Design/Build Remodeling* by Linda Case, Victoria Downing, and Wendy Jordan for details on making an architect alliance work.

Bankers. Homeowners often need home equity loans or second mortgages to complete their remodeling plans. Bankers may meet with the homeowner early in the remodeling process and can point these prospects in your direction. Ask your banker what information he or she needs to feel comfortable referring the bank's clients your company.

Landscape companies. Many landscapers work with the same types of clients that you do. By sharing resources and lists, both companies can benefit at a lower cost. In addition, bringing in a landscaper to work with your clients broadens the services you're able to offer. In just one year, a Midwestern remodeler did

$500,000 of work that was referred by a landscaper with whom he had an alliance. By the same token, the remodeler referred $300,000 of work back to the landscaper.

Builders. Builders who don't do remodeling often are asked for referrals. Many of them don't know remodelers whom they trust. See if you can find a builder who serves the same socioeconomic and geographic niche you do and create an alliance with the company.

Specialty companies. We call remodelers that focus on siding, roofing, windows, sunrooms, or decks, or that focus solely on kitchens and baths, specialty companies. Most of these companies don't do structural remodeling, so they need to work with another company when their clients need those services. For instance, many kitchen and bath specialists will not handle structural changes. They need you to frame or move walls, but they still want to design and build the new kitchen and install the appliances.

Marketers predict that these alliances and teams are the trend of the future. The hardest work is finding a client. If your ally has a client that they can refer to you for additional services, you both win.

TESTIMONIALS PACK A WALLOP

An old saying goes, "If you say something about your company, it's a claim. But if someone else says something about your company, it's a fact."

One way to let your prospects know about the quality of your services is to let your previous customers do the talking for you through the generous use of testimonial quotes. A statement about the wonderful work your company does has much more impact if it comes from a client than if it comes from you. Most clients are delighted to write a note or letter about your company if they're asked. It's your job to ask.

When the project is finished and the clients tell you how happy they are, simply say, "I'm glad that you're happy with the project. We certainly enjoyed working with you. It would be a great help to me and my company if I could let my prospective clients know how happy you are with the work we did. Would you mind taking a minute to write a short note about your experience with us?" Typically, the clients say yes in an instant. If they don't, that's a sign that they're not really all that happy and you'd better dig to find out why.

Most people have good intentions to write you a testimonial, but many of them simply forget. However, once they've agreed to do it, it's easy to remind them with a quick telephone call. Here's what you might say: "Hello, Mrs. Smith? I just wanted to call to make sure that everything is all right with the new addition. Is everything working as expected? Great. Please be sure to call us if you need anything or have any problems. Oh, by the way, did you have a chance to drop us that note we talked about? Would you mind? Thanks a lot. It'll really be a great help."

Usually one reminder is enough and soon you'll receive a wonderful letter that can be turned into a powerful marketing tool. A collection of letters from happy clients clearly demonstrates that your company delivers what you promise. There's no stronger marketing tool than a series of letters from satisfied clients. Remember to thank each person who sends you a testimonial letter or note.

Be sure the testimonial is glowing. The very best testimonial letters state what the buyer was concerned about initially and then explain how the work you did and the way you did it convinced them they made an excellent choice when they selected your company.

Here are some ways to use testimonials to market your company:

▸ Send prospective or new clients a copy of the letter with a cover letter saying:

> "Every once in a while, we receive a letter that we just have to share. This is just one of those occasions. Please take a moment to read what Mrs. Smith has to say about her experience with our company.
>
> "We promise great service and a quality product and, as Mrs. Smith knows, we deliver. You can be sure that you will receive exactly the same high-quality workmanship on your project."

▸ Use a strong sentence from the letter as a headline for an ad.

▸ Send copies of two or three letters and information introducing the company to your prospects before your first meeting.

- Be sure your copies look great. Carefully copy black-and-white letters on a standard black-and-white copier. Use a color copier to copy a letter written on colored paper or with colored ink. It's worth the extra effort and cost.

- Include a copy of the letter in your leave-behind packet of information.

- Frame a good copy of the letter and hang it on the wall of your office.

- Use segments of a series of letters in brochures and other marketing pieces.

- A quote from a client testimonial on the front of a simple black-and-white postcard makes a hard-hitting but inexpensive job site marketing piece.

- Quotes can be blown up and used as signage on a home show booth.

- Include copies of the letters in your presentation book.

- Use a testimonial quote on every page of your web site.

Testimonial letters and quotes from clients are one of the strongest ways to get your message across. People are more likely to believe another customer than they are the owner of the company. So ask every client for a letter and start collecting a quantity of wonderful words about your company. You'll never find a stronger selling tool.

CIRCLE OF INFLUENCE PROGRAM MARKETING PLAN AND BUDGET

Marketing guru Jay Conrad Levinson, author of *Guerrilla Marketing,* recommends spending 60% of your marketing resources on this segment. We agree. This is the most important part of your marketing plan. We've filled in some "must do's." Be sure you have a widely diversified, creative, and fun program here before you move onto something else.

TACTICS/EFFORTS COST

Thank-you cards to referrers $ ———————

4 to 7 contacts with Circle of Influence $ ———————

———————————————— $ ———————

———————————————— $ ———————

———————————————— $ ———————

———————————————— $ ———————

———————————————— $ ———————

———————————————— $ ———————

TOTAL BUDGET $ ———————

part four

REACHING OUT TO TARGETED PROSPECTS

We've been talking about your Circle of Influence. Now let's focus on prospects. One way to think about this is to picture the concentric circles a stone makes when it's tossed into a pond. The innermost circle is that Circle of Influence. It's your strongest area of marketing. The next strongest area is the next circle—your prospects.

Prospects are people who fit your predetermined target market.

Say you typically work on homes ranging from $200,000 to $300,000 in value that are owned by professionals aged 45 to 65 who have combined household incomes of $100,000 or more. If you want to continue working with that audience, your prospects are those people who fit within these same or similar parameters.

If you do historic renovations under $100,000 on commercial buildings, your prospects may be owners or managers of those special buildings. If you do insurance restoration projects, your prospects would be insurance company agents and adjusters in addition to homeowners. If you specialize in light commercial, your target market is completely different than that of a company focusing on residential home improvements.

To best target your company's prospects, know what market you're targeting. Then determine the best ways to reach this profitable audience.

Take a moment to review the work you did earlier in identifying your target market. Keep that audience in mind as you read about the various tactics you can use to reach them. While many of these tactics focus on homeowners, most are easily adaptable to other markets.

Here are some ideas for reaching prospects that many remodeling companies use successfully. Add your own strategies to create a complete prospect marketing plan.

MARKETING TO PROSPECTS NEAR YOUR CURRENT JOBS

If your company specializes in residential projects, the people who own homes surrounding your current jobs are excellent prospects. They probably share the same basic demographics, may be similar in age, and have incomes similar to your current customers.

Don't miss the opportunity to attract business from these homeowners. A well thought-out program will help establish your company name in the neighborhood and encourage these prospects to keep an eye on your progress. For many remodelers, this is a mainstay of their lead generation program.

Your job site is like a factory showroom right there in the neighborhood. By drawing attention to the job site with signs, mailings, and other tactics, you'll have the opportunity to show off your company's construction skills and your staff's professionalism. Remember to talk to your subcontractors about the importance of representing your company professionally as well. The entire neighborhood will be watching, so keeping your job sites clean and neat is a must! Here are some popular strategies for job site marketing.

GRAB THEIR ATTENTION WITH GREAT-LOOKING JOB SITE SIGNS

A great-looking job site sign in a customer's yard tells the neighborhood that your company is working for people just like them. You're that good! Site signs are a proven, effective marketing tactic that produce quality leads at a very low price. A New England remodeler saw leads jump 20% after he revamped his signage into oversized, bright, and well-designed signs. If yours aren't pulling in leads now, they may need help.

Site Sign Tips:

- Signage should be neat, clean, and display your company logo, telephone number, web site, and a short tagline describing the company or list of services offered.

- Always use your company colors and logo on your job signs. Your signage supplements your other neighborhood marketing tactics, so it's important that the neighbors recognize that all of the materials are coming from the same company.

- If your company name doesn't explain what kind of work you do, be sure to add a tagline such as "Another Beautiful Remodeling Project by Smith Construction."

- Have your signs printed on both sides and place them perpendicular to the street to make them easier for drivers to read.

- Use an attractive, substantial sign holder. Your sign should reflect the high-quality workmanship your company is known for. If your company is a design/build firm, design your site signage to demonstrate your creative flair. Increasingly, remodelers are designing outstanding signs with open work and turned wood standards and are highlighting them with lighting and plants. Let your imagination soar!

- Add a tube or box for promotional materials like many real estate agents do and place well-designed informational flyers inside. This is an easy way for interested homeowners to learn additional information about your company.

- Some neighborhoods don't allow signs to be posted on job sites. Inventive remodelers add colorful signage to company trailers and trucks that act as site signs while they're on the job.

Remodelers are some of the world's most creative people. Be sure to use some of that creativity on your very visible job site signs!

For more ideas, details and pricing options on job-site signs, check out these web sites: *www.dee-sign.com, www.fastsigns.com,* and *www.ppisign.com.*

 STREETSMARTS

◀ *Creative Contracting, Inc., in North Wales, Pa., uses a standard job site sign format and enhances it with company colors and an easy-to-see logo.*

◀ *Potomac Builders, Inc., in Alexandria, Va., incorporates a tagline to communi-cate the services it offers.*

◄

Out of the Woods Construction and Cabinetry, Inc., in Arlington, Mass., created this elaborate sign to draw attention to a major project while matching the home's architectural details.

■ ■ ■

HANGING YOUR MESSAGE: USING DOOR KNOB HANGERS

Door knob hangers are marketing pieces that are hung on the door knobs of homes immediately surrounding a job site. They can be used as part of a canvassing program or as a free-standing means of generating telephone calls to your office. Some studies show that homeowners don't like materials attached to their houses, but many remodelers attest to their value as lead-getters.

If you use door hangers as a free-standing marketing tactic, target at least 30 to 50 houses surrounding the job site. Make sure the door hanger includes your logo, lists the services you offer, and includes a call-to-action such as "Call today to schedule your free consultation." Hangers can be created especially for your company or can be ordered from an office supply company like NEBS (*www.NEBS.com*).

Be sure to check with the manufacturers of the products you use. Many of them have beautiful, professionally designed and printed marketing materials. The quality is high and the cost is typically quite low because everyone who purchases the materials shares in the investment to produce them. You may be surprised by the array of marketing materials available from manufacturers.

This is a sample of the attractive, full-color door knob hangers produced by the CertainTeed Corporation (*www.Certainteed.com*).

Let Your Feet Do the Walking: Effective Canvassing

Simply put, canvassing is selling door-to-door. The goal is to talk to a homeowner face-to-face with the objective of setting an appointment for a company salesperson to do a full presentation in the next few days. This marketing technique has been around forever, and some companies find it a very effective component of their overall marketing program.

Canvassing is fairly easy when it's done on a small scale with the production manager or company owner talking with homeowners who live near a job site. However, when it's done on a large scale, it is a difficult form of marketing that requires professional canvassers who can handle constant rejection. It's a technique most suited to the lower and middle class markets and to specialty products. But make no mistake about it—canvassing sells.

Canvassing Tips:

▶ "Cold" canvassing, in which professional canvassers hit random neighborhoods, is used primarily by specialty contractors. Most canvassing programs concentrate on canvassing areas around a job site; the job is used as a point of reference for the company.

▶ One canvassing manager canvasses the same neighborhood monthly but rotates the canvassers so that people see a new face.

▶ If a canvasser cannot set a sales presentation appointment, he or she can leave behind brochures and marketing materials—product literature, company information, perhaps a magnet or specialty item—and suggest that the homeowner take a look at the neighborhood job.

- If the homeowner isn't home when the canvasser visits, he or she can use a doorknob hanger or plastic bag to leave behind promotional materials that deliver the marketing message.

- The most common times for canvassing are late in the afternoon, early evening hours, and Saturday, because that is when homeowners are most likely to be at home.

- Once an appointment has been set, someone should confirm the appointment with the homeowner the day before the presentation so the salesperson won't waste his or her time. Statistics show that 30% of prospects cancel their appointments during the appointment confirmation, even if the person calling attempts to resell the prospect. Try your best to keep the appointment alive, but if you can't, it's still better to find out about the cancellation before the salesperson takes the time to go to the appointment.

- The quality of the leads is relatively low; a salesperson can anticipate selling 20 to 40% of his or her appointments.

As you can see, canvassing is a very specialized marketing tool!

STREET SMARTS

Advertisements and promotions work great for some companies, but when Swimme & Son Building Contractors, Inc., in Elizabeth City, N.C., wants to make a sale, its employees make house calls. Using a combination of marketing and canvassing techniques, the company produces top-quality leads in a short amount of time.

After sending postcards to approximately 600 homes in a neighborhood, neatly dressed crew members went door to door armed with clipboards and materials offering free estimates on home improvement projects.

"They knocked on every door and asked to set up an appointment to come back and give an estimate on siding, gutter, and window work," says Mark Swimme, company owner and president. "There was no pressure to buy. They were just making appointments."

Following a carefully prepared script that informed homeowners that the company was doing work in the community and would be happy to address their home improvement needs, a crew of three booked 10 appointments in five hours. In addition to their hourly rate, crew members were paid an extra five dollars per lead, and the brochures they left in people's homes could very well produce additional leads in weeks to come.

■ ■ ■

A Sample Canvassing Script

"Hi, I'm Bill Peters of Blanchfield Exterior Renovations. Did you notice that we're re-siding the home next door? I wanted to let you know that we try to disrupt the neighborhood as little as possible.

"Our company is a specialist in exterior home improvements. In fact, we provide top-quality replacement windows, gutters, and vinyl siding. Have you been thinking of improving your home or saving money with more energy efficiency? Well, while we're in your area, I'd love to talk to you about what we offer. I'm setting appointments in the neighborhood on Tuesday and Thursday. I could show you how we can transform your house at that time. Which day would be better for you?"

If the prospects don't want to make an appointment:

"Here's a brochure about our company for when you decide that it's time to improve your home. By the way, would any of your neighbors like to have information on our services? Thanks so much for your time, and please call if there's anything we can do for you. Goodbye."

Tricks of the Trade:

▸ The person you choose as canvassing manager can make or break the program. Canvassing is a business within your business and must be continually managed and controlled.

▸ You'll need a constant source of part-time workers. College students often fit the bill.

▸ Canvassers used to be paid entirely on commission, based on how many leads they generated. Now, to motivate them, many canvassers are paid a low minimum wage plus an additional commission per lead.

▸ A canvasser in an urban area can knock on 100 doors an hour. The canvasser will probably set one appointment per hour on average.

Tips for Small-Scale Canvassing Programs:

▸ Use your existing staff, high school students, or your own teenage children to canvass a few homes surrounding the job. Make sure they wear uniforms or shirts with your company logo.

▸ Small-scale programs using your own personnel tend to be a softer-sell and less high pressure—therefore, homeowners are likely to be more receptive.

JOB SITE MAILINGS

Another way to reach the prospects living around a job site is to use the mail. Often easy-to-implement, this tactic produces high-quality leads. The mailing can be as simple as a letter or as complex as a multi-piece mailing with an attached business reply card.

Most remodeling companies use either a series of letters on their own company letterhead or a combination of letters and post cards. Since mailings can reach more people inexpensively, plan on contacting up to 100 homes surrounding each job.

Kelly Eggers, marketing director and co-owner of Remodeling Designs, Inc., in Dayton, Ohio, uses job site mailings as a mainstay of the company's marketing program. For some time, Eggers sent customized postcards to 60 to 300 homes surrounding Remodeling Designs' best jobs. This year, the company will use an oversized, 6"x 11" postcard that features photos of four completed projects. "We used a larger postcard for a special mailing and received a much-better-than-average response," says Kelly, "so we're revamping our job site mailings to go that way, too."

While the immediate response rate is 1 to 2%, which is typical of most direct mail campaigns, Kelly says, "the cards put our company name and logo in front of a very desirable audience."

■ ■ ■

Job site mailing programs work—when they get done! Many remodelers try—and fail—to do these mailings from their office. They do not have adequate manpower to find the addresses, manually address the envelopes or postcards, and mail the pieces.

Find an office service or mailing service subcontractor in your area that can produce the address labels and mail the pieces on a regular basis. You may pay a little more, but you'll guarantee that this part of your marketing program actually happens. A low-priced, part-time employee also can be a wonderful resource to implement a job site mailing program.

Sample Job Site Mailing Campaign Schedule

PROJECT: *An addition that will be completed within three months.*

First mailing: Postcard sent two weeks before the job begins.

Second mailing: Copy of company newsletter with cover letter sent two weeks after job has begun.

Third mailing: Second postcard mailed six weeks before job is completed.

Fourth mailing: Letter from president sent two weeks before job is completed.

SAMPLE JOB SITE LETTER I

To be sent out at the beginning of a project within one week of construction starting.

Dear Neighbor,

Have you noticed what your neighbors on (street name) are up to? After careful investigation, they chose to remodel with (Your Company Name). We have started construction and invite you to watch our progress.

Perhaps you have been thinking about a remodeling project that would add value to your home and pleasure to your life. Many homeowners don't know where to start to make their wishes a reality. It can be difficult to find the right remodeling company to help you through the process. But you can't go wrong with (YOUR COMPANY NAME).

We (OR YOUR COMPANY NAME) offer extensive experience in creative design and quality construction. As an experienced general contractor, we will work with you to incorporate your ideas and ours into a project that fits your home, lifestyle, and budget.

If you're ready to talk about exciting remodeling possibilities for your home, call 000-000-0000 today to arrange a (FREE DESIGN CONSULTATION) (MEETING) (SHOWROOOM APPOINTMENT). We look forward to hearing from you soon!

> Cordially,
> (Your Name)
> (Company Name)

P.S. There's never been a better time to remodel. If you'd like to discuss your ideas with a professional, call us today!

SAMPLE JOB SITE LETTER 2

To be sent out halfway through the project.

Dear Neighbor,

Your neighbor's remodeling project is really taking shape! We are nearing completion and they are delighted. We hope you have enjoyed watching our progress.

Perhaps you've been thinking about how nice it would be to live in a "new" house. You can create that feeling with affordable, creative remodeling. Remodeling or adding onto your existing home is a wonderful option to moving because you can maintain your neighborhood friendships and all of your local resources. In addition, you will be adding value and equity to your property.

If you'd like to talk about how remodeling can improve your home, call us. We offer extensive experience in creative design and quality construction. As an experienced general contractor, we will work with you to design and construct a home that fits your lifestyle and your budget.

If you're ready to talk about remodeling possibilities for your house, call 000-000-0000 today for a free (CONSULTATION) (ESTIMATE). We look forward to hearing from you.

Cordially,
(Your Name)

P.S. It's not easy choosing the right remodeler, but if you're looking for professional, knowledgeable craftspeople, our clients say you can't do better than (YOUR COMPANY NAME).

SAMPLE JOB SITE LETTER 3

To be sent out just before you leave the job site.

Hello,

The project we have been working on in your area has recently been completed. Your neighbors are thoroughly satisfied and pleased that they chose us as their remodeling company. As your neighbors will tell you, planning is the first important step for any remodeling project. We can help walk you through the process, assist you with design and selection of materials, and help you prepare for the actual construction phase. With some careful planning and great attention to detail, your dream can become a reality.

Now that you've seen the difference we can make, it's time to call us to discuss plans for your home. We'll work with you to incorporate your ideas and ours into a project that fits your home, lifestyle, and budget. Isn't it time to have the home you've always dreamed of? Call us today at 000-000-0000 to discuss your ideas and to schedule your free (DESIGN CONSULTATION) (MEETING) (SHOWROOM VISIT).

Cordially,
(Your Name)

P.S. With our years of experience, we can help you maximize your budget to get the most value for every dollar you invest.

Call 000-000-0000 today to talk over your plans.

JOB SITE POSTCARDS

An alternative to mailing letters is to use a postcard in place of one of the letters. Postcards are effective communicators because few people can resist turning them over to see the message—they're already "open."

If you're planning to send more than 200 at a time, you're eligible to use the bulk mail option. Check with your mailing house to see if bulk mail will save money. If so, be sure to print the postcard with the bulk mail indicia.

WHO DO I SEND IT TO? CREATING A JOB SITE MAILING LIST

Here are some ideas on how to compile a mailing list of neighbors around each job.

1. Use your city's criss-cross directory, which is available at most local libraries and can be purchased online. This easy-to-use directory tells you who lives at which address. It can also be purchased in hard copy format or, in some areas, in a CD-ROM format that your computer can use to quickly pull up names, addresses, and telephone numbers. (If you purchase the hard copy, enter the names and addresses into your computer to easily print envelopes and personalized letters.)

   The CD-ROM criss-cross directories can be purchased at *www.haines.com* and *www.experiam.com;* each of these sites will update the programs monthly for one year after purchase.

   Another excellent resource is the U.S. Postal Service web site; it has a page that caters specifically to people who want to create a successful direct mailing list. For more information, visit the web site at *www.usps.com/directmail.*

2. An alternative is to drive through the neighborhood and make note of the house numbers and street names.

3. Plan ahead so that you produce sets of labels all at one time for each mailing you will do.

4. If you don't have in-house capabilities, hire a secretarial or office service firm to help you with the actual mailing. For a fee, they can input the names and addresses, print the letters, stuff the envelopes or put labels on the postcards, add the postage, and drop them at the Post Office.

STREETSMARTS

Melissa Connelly of R.L. Connelly & Company, Inc., in Atlanta, Ga., uses *Criss-Cross Plus*, a service from *Haines & Company, Inc.*, to create targeted mailing lists for her large-volume company. For less than $500 a year, Melissa receives an updated CD-ROM with information on thousands of homeowners. "It takes just moments to target the areas we want to hit," she says. "In addition to the address and homeowner name, the information also includes some demographic information that helps us choose exactly the right homes for us." Connelly & Company then sends personalized letters that are more likely to grab the homeowner's attention than generic mailers.

■ ■ ■

▼

GRAB 'EM AT THE DOOR

One remodeler made a big splash in the neighborhoods in which the company worked by placing disposable door mats with a large company logo in front of homes surrounding his job. The door mat was accompanied by a letter explaining that the company would be doing a remodeling project nearby that might generate dirt in the street, so the remodeler hoped the doormat would help keep the dirt out of the neighbors' homes. An inexpensive but creative job site marketing tactic!

▲

TARGET PROSPECTS WITH DIRECT MAIL

Direct mail is one of the most efficient methods of reaching many prospects, but it can be an expensive failure if it's not done correctly. Even if highly successful, you can only expect a 1 to 2% return rate.

Direct mail is defined as live, personal selling translated into the print medium. It can be one way to generate a high volume of leads. However, because you're reaching prospects who may have never heard of your company, the leads tend to be of lower quality than those produced by many of the tactics we've discussed previously.

 STREETSMARTS

Direct mail is a direct success for Classic Remodeling in Charleston, S.C. The company sends postcards that highlight its remodeling services, projects, and client testimonials to a target audience of homeowners who have annual incomes of more than $500,000.

"The postcards we've sent out have done relatively well for us," says Bob Fleming, president of Classic Remodeling. "We immediately landed several jobs that we wouldn't have gotten otherwise."

The company also mails tri-fold brochures to potential clients in specific neighborhoods in which it prefers to work. The full-color brochures are mailed in clear envelopes to grab homeowners' attention.

"It's not just one piece. Every one we do—the ads, the signs, the postcards, and the brochures—all fit together," Fleming says. "The postcards and the brochures tie the whole picture together. We have gotten linked to people who said they were already thinking of using us for their remodeling projects. Then they received the postcard or the brochure and gave us a call."

■ ■ ■

Direct mail can be expensive. It's a tricky medium to use successfully and the chance for failure is quite high. Think of how you handle your direct mail (often called "junk" mail). Each day you get a pile of mail, sort through it quickly to pull out the items to save, and then throw away—unopened—the material you don't want. Your company's direct mail must somehow bypass that first cut into the trash can!

Many remodeling companies use direct mail to target specific neighborhoods with special promotions: winter savings, new product announcements, start spring remodeling now, or remodel before the holidays. These special promotions help attract work during slower periods.

THE TARGETED MAILING LIST

It's been said that the success of a direct mail campaign depends on the quality of the list of people receiving the mailing. Any mailing list you use should contain the names and addresses of those people who have similar demographics as your customers.

To reach residential remodeling prospects, you can use your own in-house list of prospects compiled over the years, create a mailing list of the members of the various organizations you belong to, focus on homes in the neighborhoods in which you are already working (as already discussed under Job Site Mailings), or purchase a list of prospects from a mail house.

If you purchase a mailing list from a mail list vendor, you can define exactly who you'd like to receive your piece by such parameters as prospect age, zip code, number of years at a given address, household income, home age and value, number of children, etc. The more definers you add, the costlier but more targeted the list will be.

Most mail list vendors rent the lists for one-time use. Mailing lists are often "salted" with insider names so that the list company can track the mailed piece and discern if the list has been used without permission. Most mailing lists contain some information that is no longer correct, giving you some "dead" contacts (10% is common). A higher percentage of poor contacts means that the list has been poorly maintained and won't be worth the money.

To reach business-to-business prospects, focus on associations or publications that serve that particular niche. These organizations typically sell mailing lists. If, for example, your company specializes in creating beautiful restaurants, you may want to contact the National Restaurant Association to inquire about purchasing a member list, or find the top industry publication and purchase its mailing list. If your company remodels apartments and you want to target property managers, talk to the local property management association or the publication serving this market.

Most remodeling business owners prefer to stay away from the local assessor's office. But not Jerry T. Kelly, president of GT Kelly, Inc., in Lenox Dale, Mass. Jerry actually enjoys visiting the local assessor. After all, it's a great way for him to develop leads for his company.

Jerry obtains locally generated mailing lists from the assessors' offices and uses those lists to market his company. The information is in the public domain and is available through the Freedom of Information Act. For a small fee, Jerry receives the lists in writing or on a disc.

"These lists are highly accurate. Nobody has information like the local assessor and knows where everybody is," Jerry says. "They are a great source. When the mail goes out, the phone starts ringing. We get a great response. It does work."

Once he has the lists, Jerry can import the information into a software program such as Excel and sort his leads by name, address, property value, or by other criteria and start advertising to them.

■ ■ ■

THE PIECE YOU MAIL

The second most important part of the direct mail advertising after the quality of the mailing list is the quality of what is mailed. Here are some guidelines:

▸ The envelope is an important part of the message. Think of how many pieces of mail you throw out without opening. How can you get the prospect to open that envelope? Experts say that you can increase the number of people who open and read the mailing simply by telling them to open it—"Open to find out how you can…" or "Read inside to learn more!" The more the envelope looks like "real" mail, the more likely it is to be opened. Is it addressed to the actual name or just to "Homeowner"?

▸ Has the piece been sent first class with a stamp (which makes it more likely to be opened) or is it bulk mail? Bulk mail can be used for 200 pieces of mail or more and can drastically cut postage costs. However, if you're mailing bulk mail, remember that the Post Office reserves the right to hold the mail in its facilities for up to two weeks. If you're mailing any information with a timely message, you may want to use first class postage for a more rapid delivery.

▸ Once the envelope is opened, you have five to eight seconds to grab the reader's attention. Only 10 to 15% of people who receive direct mail read the copy at all. Your offer must be quickly read and understood.

Prospects read your mail in three stages:

First they scan it for relevancy. In this stage they are reading the attention-getters—the headlines, picture captions, and subheads.

If they continue, they read with interest but have no intention yet of taking action.

The 5% who have made it this far are now reading to confirm their decision to move forward. At this point, they have read all or most of the copy in the letter.

▸ Two of the most important parts of the direct mail letter are the headline (yes, even a letter should have a headline) and the P.S. at the bottom. These are normally the first parts the reader scans. Use them positively and wisely. This is a great place to repeat your call-to-action. ("Call us today!")

▸ Consider a self-mailer—a piece that's sent without an envelope. Usually folded pieces, self-mailers avoid the expense of using an envelope but still require a strong, intriguing statement on the outside to encourage prospects to open them.

▸ People buy solutions, not products. They don't buy for function; they buy for emotional reasons. Always emphasize benefits, not features. The prospect is always asking "What's in it for me?" It's your job to answer this question.

GETTING THE RESPONSE

Be sure to include a call-to-action in every direct mail piece you create. Urge the prospect to respond today. Some companies create a sense of urgency by mentioning a limited time to respond, a special offer (a free microwave oven with every kitchen installed by September 25), or free information (*100 Ways To Double Your Storage Space* or *Increase Profit with Creative Restaurant Design*). For your call-to-action, first decide what you want them to do, and tell them how to do it. Do you want them to call for an appointment? Visit your showroom? Call for additional information?

Readers are more likely to respond if you reduce their risk of doing so. Write about a no-obligation appointment, or "no salesperson will call," or "satisfaction guaranteed." Make it easy for them to take action by prominently displaying a toll-free number, enclosing a self-addressed envelope, or attaching a business reply card.

TRICKS OF THE TRADE

▸ As we mentioned earlier, success in direct mail is defined as a 1% or better response rate. If you want to get 50 responses, you must mail at least 5,000 pieces. To be frank, few people even reach the 1% response rate. To be realistic, plan to mail 7,000 to 10,000 pieces if you're looking for 50 to 100 responses.

- The best prospects are those who have a history of responding to direct mail. There are people who respond to mailed advertising and those that don't—and a wide range of people in between. Catalog mailers know that if they purchase lists of buyers from other catalog companies, they'll be advertising to direct mail responders. For the contractor, this means that if you sell new products or services, always think of previous direct mail buyers from your company as a very "hot" list.

- If you send a large quantity of mailers, be prepared for a large number of responses. Do you have the personnel to handle the calls? If you're too busy to handle the prospects who call, you'll be wasting money as well as alienating possible customers. Instead, do the mailing in smaller phases to make sure you can handle the inquiries.

- Include a response card that the recipients can mail back to you for more information or to set an appointment. A business reply permit can be purchased from the U.S. Post Office and printed on the reply card. It allows the prospect to drop the card in the mail without paying for postage. You'll pick up the postage, but only for those cards returned to you. This technique will increase your response rate from interested prospects.

- To build your database with prospects, create a secondary response mechanism, such as a tip sheet or small brochure on *Planning Your Remodeling Project* or *How to Choose a Remodeler* (these are available from many industry associations at a low price). Offer the tip sheet or brochure to recipients free of charge. (Remember, "FREE" is one of the most powerful words to use in direct mail.)

- When these quality prospects call in, add them to your prospect database and continue to market to them. If they're interested in the brochure, chances are they're also very interested in remodeling their homes.

- Consider exchanging mailing lists with a non-competitive company such as a landscape firm, pool company, real estate agent, or an insurance agent. Make sure its customers' demographics are similar to your customers'. If you're selling to upscale homeowners and the non-competitive company works with blue-collar homeowners, the mix won't fit and the mailing will fail. However, matching up with a company with similar customers will save you money on reaching a broad range of prospects.

  If you work for customers who aren't homeowners, be creative in how you might team up with another vendor selling to the same market for the same sort of important impact.

- Studies show that the best months for direct mail are generally January, February, October, and August. The next best months are November, December, September, and July. The poorest months are April, May, June, and March. No information is available about the best times for remodeling companies to use direct mail.

- Test large direct mail campaigns with a smaller number of pieces. Whenever possible, do double testing—check the results from two different mailing pieces or two different neighborhoods against one another. Testing should always include at least enough mailing pieces to generate a minimum of 20 responses. If your experience has been a 1% rate of return, your test size will need to be at least 2,000 pieces.

As with all marketing programs, measure, measure, measure! Measuring the response is even more important with high-risk, high-cost methods like direct mail. Each mailing should be individually analyzed to determine the effectiveness of the mailing list used, the piece sent, the number of leads generated, and the number of sales generated. Constant monitoring is the only way to educate yourself about what really works for you in direct mail.

POSTCARD DECKS

Postcard decks combine advertising pieces from many different companies into a single package. This package is then mailed to a specific target audience. This approach is less expensive for each participant than doing the mailing alone, and provides the homeowner with a variety of appealing marketing messages in each package.

John Murphy, owner of Murphy Bros. Building & Remodeling Co. in Blaine, Minn., participates in a postcard deck created by R.S.V.P. Publications *(www.rsvppublications.com)*. R.S.V.P. creates glossy, full-color postcards that are sent to affluent homeowners across the country. The participants in the deck can choose just the geographic areas they feel are right for their company. The publication company can handle design and printing in addition to the mailing. And it limits the companies in each category to restrict competitive companies from participating. "We signed up for the addition/general remodeling category," says John. "There were other remodelers there who were focusing on kitchens and baths or windows and doors. No one directly competed with what we offered."

Here are the Murphy Brothers results:

- Three mailings to 100,000 people each
- An investment of just over $14,000 dollars for the three mailings
- 218 leads
- 2 feasibility studies sold for projects worth $55,000
- 5 design/build agreements sold for projects worth $655,750
- 4 construction contracts sold for jobs totaling $434,404 in contract value
- 83 prospects are still pending.

John says, "We anticipated the revenue that will be directly attributable to this mailing will reach $1.5 million. With that kind of return, we'll be using this marketing tool far into the future!"

▲ *This attractive full-color postcard includes a special offer for the company's design services.*

NETWORKING:
PERSON-TO-PERSON LEAD GENERATION

While direct marketing tactics can and do produce leads for your business, there's another, softer method that you'll find produces some of the highest quality leads available: Networking.

Networking is simply building relationships with people who can help your business by bringing direct sales or by sending referral leads.

Meeting and talking with people may seem like a natural activity that doesn't need a system. However, experts agree you can maximize your impact with strategy. Here are tips on how to begin your networking efforts:

‣ Create a high profile for your company within the community. Join a local organization—perhaps the local Chamber of Commerce, the Rotary Club, or the Elks—and then participate. Show up for meetings and volunteer for a committee. Your professionalism and caring attitude will shine through and affect the impression you're making on an influential group in the community.

‣ Volunteer for a specific project. This could be the annual United Way fundraising drive, or chairing the committee to put a new roof on your church. By donating your time to a good cause, you're demonstrating that you care about more than money. And we all know that the good you do now will be returned to you tenfold in the future.

‣ Take a business associate—maybe a supplier, someone from your industry association, or another acquaintance from town—to breakfast or lunch once a month. You can't lose. At a minimum you'll have an influential friend of the company, but leads are also likely to result. Cross-referring is an excellent way to thank businesspeople for sending referrals to you.

- Ask to be appointed to the town planning board or board of education building maintenance committee. Towns need individuals who are experienced in zoning, codes, etc. to serve on boards of zoning adjustment, planning boards, or recreation committees. Boards of education also can use expert input for dealing with building maintenance and buying replacement and new products and materials.

- Suppliers are a steady source of referrals. Take them out to lunch and ask for their advice on how to make your company stronger. They'll be flattered and you'll receive some wonderful input from people who know what's going on in the industry.

- Ask your employees to participate in the networking effort by representing your company at meetings. Encourage them to ask for referrals in their own organizations like the PTA, the ski club, the little league parents, etc.

- Thank each and every referrer with a handwritten card. Those who provide leads frequently deserve a bottle of wine, a flower arrangement, or some type of special gift.

- Introduce yourself innovatively. You meet dozens of people each day—people who could be your company's customers or who could refer your company. To pique their interest and create an opportunity to tell them more about the services you offer, develop a compelling statement to use when introducing your company.

This statement, also called an audio logo, elevator speech, or 30-second commercial, should provide a quick answer to the question, "What do you do?" It should be short, compelling, and mention the audience you serve. The main goal? Your introduction should elicit the response, "Tell me more!"

Remember, you are NOT answering the question, "Who are you?" The common dead-end answer to that question is:

"I'm a remodeler." With that unimaginative response, you leave the client with nothing to lead into a further conversation.

Here are some examples of compelling statements:

"Our company helps homeowners throughout Howard County turn their house into their dream home."

"We work with families in Bethesda to create homes that their kids want to bring their friends to."

- Have an agenda. As you drive or walk to the get-together, define what you have to give others and what you want to get out of this meeting. Be up front about your desire to do business with the people you meet. However, when the conversation moves to the "doing business together" stage, set an appointment to discuss it in depth in a business setting.

- Listen generously. Keep an ear tuned for what you can do for each person. Use open-ended questions that can't be answered with a yes or no or one word. Questions that start with how, why, what, or "tell me about" lead your partner into self-revealing answers.

- Give valuable information. Since your conversation has given you insights into your new friend's interests, follow up with introductions to people you know he or she will enjoy. Clip and send pertinent articles or invite the person to an association meeting he or she will find interesting.

- Give out your business cards only after you've formed a conversational bond. The game is not how many business cards you can hand out, but how many solid connections you can make.

Learning networking know-how is easy and effective, but too few remodelers realize the effect of powerful relationships. Remodelers who want their companies to succeed need to make networking a priority.

Sue McDowell truly understands the importance of networking. As co-owner of McDowell, Inc., of St. Charles, in St. Charles, Ill., her participation in several community and business groups have put her remodeling company on the map in this mid-sized city.

"Creating business through networking is a long time investment," she says. "The key to success with this type of marketing is to go into it with the attitude that you are going to help the organization by giving your time and expertise. Don't join an organization if your only goal is getting business. As you participate and help, your fellow members begin to know and trust you. They form a perception of your company that is mirrored by the way you act."

McDowell, Inc., belongs to a variety of community organizations including the Chamber of Commerce, the Downtown Revitalization Committee, and the Women's Auxiliary of the Hospital.

Sue says, "The more organizations you join, the wider the cross section of people you'll reach and the more awareness you'll create for the company."

Membership in these organizations is paid for from the McDowell marketing budget and requires an investment of less than $5,000. The time invested, however, is a different story. "To participate adequately in one or two community organizations—attending monthly meetings, going to the monthly mixer, and participating actively on at least one committee—expect to invest at least four to six hours each month," Sue says.

The McDowells have seen their philanthropic efforts pay off hugely. Sue and her husband, Bob, have received numerous awards and accolades for their extraordinary involvement in the community. These awards are then run in the local newspapers, which gives the company a huge publicity boost.

Also, due to her efforts on behalf of the city, Sue was recognized as a business leader and was recruited for the local bank's board of directors. This assignment puts her on par with the top business people in the area—and of course this status rubs off on the company, too!

Sue says, "We knew the networking was worth it when another businessperson in town said, 'McDowell is a household name, for gosh sakes!' That's the kind of recognition we want!"

▲ *When St. Charles, Ill., needed to rebuild the small building Santa sits in each holiday season, McDowell, Inc., volunteered. Construction cost less than $500 plus the time to build it. A sign recognizing McDowell, Inc.'s efforts was highlighted the first year. Now a plaque on the Santa House continues to tell the citizens about the company. Last but not least, Bob McDowell, president of the company and main "architect" of the Santa house project, was recognized personally with a city-wide award—and again featured in a newspaper article!*

▲

TELEMARKETING:
A MARKETING SUPPLEMENT

Telemarketing is the selling of goods and services by telephone. For the remodeler, the goal is to first generate interest from the prospect, and then set an appointment for a company salesperson to do a presentation for the homeowner within the next few days.

Few remodelers had been using telemarketing due to its unpopularity with homeowners, and new restrictive laws have made large-scale telemarketing even less attractive as a direct marketing method.

But that's not to say that the telephone is no longer a good marketing tool. It can still be an important part of many marketing programs. The difference is in the approach.

Here are two workable approaches to using the telephone for marketing:

▶ Place outgoing calls to previous customers to generate repeat sales. Federal regulations give companies permission to contact customers whom they have had a business relationship with in the past 18 months. This is particularly useful for remodeling companies that produce a large number of jobs each year.

▶ Create a program that encourages consumers to call you instead. A free offer of an informational brochure, a contest, a special offer, or other item or service could attract incoming calls and give your team the opportunity to sell to these people. One a person has contacted your company, you have permission to contact them for 18 months after they have inquired about your company and/or its services unless they ask you not to call them.

The goal for both approaches is to set an appointment for a salesperson to visit the consumer. To make this as successful as possible, someone must call back and confirm the appointment the day before the salesperson is scheduled to arrive. You'll find a large percentage of the prospects will cancel at this time, even if the telemarketer tries to resell the appointment. However, once the salesperson visits, it's not uncommon to sell and close 25% to 50% of the appointments that are kept.

Even before the federal Do-Not-Call regulations went into effect in 2003, telemarketing's unpopularity with remodelers and their prospects was obvious. Large-scale, outgoing telemarketing will probably not be a viable option for your company. Check the national and state laws before you begin any telemarketing campaign.

SHOW OFF WITH AN OPEN HOUSE

A project open house is a wonderful way to show off your company's workmanship and generate very high-quality leads. Remodelers around the country have benefited from allowing prospects and customers to walk through completed jobs to touch, feel, and see the spectacular projects they've created.

You need three vital ingredients to make an open house work: a noteworthy project, welcoming clients, and a seasonable time of year. You'll be surprised at how many clients are willing, even honored, to open their homes. An added incentive might be to let them invite their friends (who are good prospects) while you provide refreshments.

Plants or an item you know your clients need make thoughtful thank-you gifts.

The fact that your clients are willing to have others come to their home to see your work says good things about you as a remodeler. Most neighbors have a hard time passing up the opportunity to see another's home, and, if they aren't ready to remodel today, they'll be ready within the next five years!

OPEN HOUSE TRICKS OF THE TRADE:

▸ Do your homework. Go to a model home in your area and observe how the home is presented to the public. Ask questions. Real estate agents can be excellent sources of information on what makes a successful open house.

▸ Be sure the project you decide to feature is in a neighborhood where you want to do additional business. Select a completed project in a highly visible area of your target neighborhood. Neighbors who have been watching the project will be eager to see the inside.

▸ Pick a Sunday in early spring or fall after the vacation season. The best time is the weekend after Labor Day. This is a great time to rekindle interest in remodeling as fall approaches.

▸ Target your marketing to include neighbors, top prospects from your company mailing list, as well as past clients. Don't use newspaper ads because they might attract thieves.

▸ Decorate the home with as many fresh flowers as your budget will allow. Be sure the house is spotless and play soft, classical music as the guests arrive.

▸ Provide adequate security inside and outside the home. Don't allow visitors to roam freely throughout the house. Post signs marking off-limit areas and escort visitors into the parts of the house being shown.

▸ Protect floors and carpets with clear plastic coverings. Some companies purchase inexpensive cloth booties from hospital supply companies. Visitors are asked to wear the booties as they tour the home. At the end of the tour, the booties are tossed into a bin where they can be recycled for the next batch of visitors.

▸ Ask every visitor to sign the register; this is the foundation of your follow-up program. Signing the register also serves as a security precaution.

- Provide simple refreshments such as colorless punch (which won't stain floors and carpets), cookies, and crackers.

- Provide plenty of handouts. These can be company brochures, specific literature about the featured project, and manufacturer literature.

- Hire a maid service for a final clean up after the open house is over. The clients will appreciate this show of consideration.

Follow up, follow up, follow up! To comply with the new rules limiting outgoing telemarketing, ask prospects to check a box on a lead sheet indicating that they would like to receive a call regarding the services your company offers. Or write everyone who visited, thanking them for coming and asking them for new business. Send each of the attendees a letter reinforcing your professionalism. Keep in contact with these people for the near future—up to two years. If they were interested enough to come to the open house, chances are they have remodeling on their minds.

JOIN A REMODELED HOME TOUR

From time to time, an organization in your community will sponsor a remodeled home tour—a selection of remodeled homes that interested people can tour for a small fee. Depending on the organization, this can be an effective way to show off your work to dozens of prospects. If you have the chance to participate, make sure you market the event yourself in addition to the sponsoring organization's marketing efforts.

A home tour is an excellent reason to contact your Circle of Influence as well as your current "hot" prospects. You can offer free or reduced-price tickets to generate increased attendance. Send a press release on the tour and your company's participation. Have company presentation materials and handouts available at your project. Your staff should dress neatly and be ready to talk to prospects about the nature of the project.

Jeb Breithaupt, of JEB Design/Build, Inc., in Shreveport, La., finds that one of his best lead generation tools is his participation in the parade of remodeled homes sponsored by his local Remodelors Council. As founder and chairman, Jeb has been very involved in the parade's development and has seen it grow. "This year, our company alone had three different homes on the tour," Jeb says.

The $1,900-per-home marketing budget is spent on:

▶ Pre-show expenses such as paint touch-up and small repairs to help the home look its best before the event

▶ Marketing materials to pass out during the tour

▶ Staff time during the parade itself. Jeb asks two staff members to represent JEB Design/Build at each home and give tours to attendees. Jeb says, "The people who visit really want the story behind it, so a staff member who is comfortable talking to stranger should be present every minute."

▶ Entry fees.

▶ Marketing materials and mailing costs for following up with prospective customers.

In 2003, more than 500 people visited the homes remodeled by JEB Design/Build, Inc. "Twenty percent of our business last year came directly from this event," says Jeb. "Plus, hundreds of people were exposed to our work and now know that we design and produce high-quality, innovative projects. It can't be beat."

BRING PROSPECTS TO YOUR DOOR WITH SPECIAL EVENTS

Another way to attract prospects to your company is to host special events that attract the kind of people you want to sell to. Some remodelers host community events in their showrooms or offices to increase awareness within a targeted group. Here are some ideas for hosted events:

▶ Chamber of Commerce or Rotary events.

▶ Offer your facility as the party location for Longaberger Baskets, Pampered Chef items, or other high-end products that are typically sold at home parties. Contact the local representative and offer your facility.

▶ Volunteer your office or showroom as a voting location.

▶ Work with the local fire station on fire safety or children's safety issues.

▶ If the local police are doing a children's fingerprinting campaign, offer to host it in your office or showroom.

▶ Arrange for an on-site broadcast of a popular radio show in your office or showroom.

There are many different ways to reach out to prospective customers and bring them into your showroom.

 STREET SMARTS

Blackdog Builders, Inc., in Salem, N.H., wanted to reach homeowners who were thinking about remodeling, so the company planned a special event around a series of four educational programs. The pivotal event was a 45-minute seminar presented by the host of a highly popular Home and Garden Television (HGTV) show, "Designing for the Sexes." The presence of celebrity Michael Payne created excitement and attracted over 120 people to the event.

In fact, the response was so great that the first program the celebrity presented was sold out, requiring a second presentation that same day.

The event, co-sponsored by the local Pella Windows contractor, was promoted primarily through newspaper ads and radio spots. Homeowners were asked to register for each of the seminars in advance. Refreshments were served and attendees were encouraged to browse through the well-appointed Blackdog showroom for remodeling ideas.

Marketing coordinator Gail Butterfield says, "Our investment of $10,000 to $12,000 was definitely worth it. The exposure in the community was huge even before the event itself. We've already planned a repeat program for next year.

■ ■ ■

PRESENTING EDUCATIONAL SEMINARS

Almost any size company can host a seminar for its target market. Educational seminars are valuable because they're designed to attract qualified prospects who are interested in the type of project your company specializes in. The presentation typically includes meaty information on:

‣ How to choose the right remodeler for your project.

‣ How to plan for the project.

‣ What to expect during construction.

Before you decide to do a seminar, consider these elements:

‣ Who will present the seminar? Are you a polished speaker? If not, plan to practice your presentation or add other speakers to bolster your abilities.

‣ What will the presentation focus on? One remodeler titled his seminar "Ten Essential Elements in Every Addition." This attracted homeowners who were planning to build an addition—the remodeler's prime customer.

‣ Don't sell "from the platform." Attendees are there to receive valuable information, not to sit through a sales pitch. They'll be sold on your company by the expertise you demonstrate during the presentation—and of course by the marketing materials available in the room or mailed to them after the seminar.

STREETSMARTS

Paul Winans, president of Winans Construction, Inc., in Oakland, Calif., has presented more than 15 educational seminars over the last five years with great success. Each seminar is hosted at a local library, which charges an affordable $100 rental fee for the space. Press releases announcing the seminars are sent to all local newspapers and Winans Construction's web site also heralds the event.

The seminar itself discusses the remodeling process with an emphasis on the particular systems that Winans uses to make it extra-special. Paul says, "We put a design/build, negotiated-contract spin on the presentation and explain exactly how we work. This gives these prospects a benchmark to compare all other remodeling companies against.

After five years, it's now a smooth process. "The only investment now is my time," says Paul. "It's a wonderful way to connect with someone who is looking for a good remodeling company. But to be successful, you have to love talking and feel comfortable doing so in front of a group of people."

■ ■ ■

More things to consider when planning a seminar:

▸ Where will it be held? Seminars can be held in public libraries, Chamber of Commerce offices, local community colleges, banks, or meeting rooms in hotels or conference centers.

▸ How many attendees do you want? Estimate the number of attendees so you can plan for seating, handouts, and refreshments (if any).

▸ How will you market the seminar? Mailings to prospects and previous customers, flyers posted at home centers, libraries, and community bulletin boards, small ads in community newspapers, ads in industry newsletters or magazines, or free listings in business and community calendars are all good ways to promote the program.

Prepare handouts that include your company name, address, web site, and telephone number. Ask each attendee to complete the guest register and provide his or her name, address, and telephone number. Be sure to ask if you can call them with more information so you can contact them via telephone after the program. Follow up with a phone call if they give you permission or send a letter within two weeks after the program. These people are highly qualified prospects, so take advantage of every opportunity to generate leads. Continue to market to this group for up to a year after the program.

Remember, if you're going to host a seminar, it's important that the entire program—from the marketing materials to the presentation itself—be organized and professional. A well-designed program will showcase your company in an extremely favorable setting, so put effort into creating a well-planned event.

 STREET SMARTS

Adam Helfman of Fairway Construction Company in Southfield, Mich., used this flyer to promote his company's two annual consumer seminars held at a local meeting facility. By securing local radio personality Glenn Haege, the host of the popular "Ask the Handyman" radio show, Helfman increased prospects' awareness of the program awareness.

Seminar marketing includes radio commercials, mailings to previous customers and prospects, and even flyers placed on the windshields of cars in parking lots. The seminars take place just a few weeks after two large local home shows in which Fairway participates. They regularly attract nearly 100 people who come to hear presentations by Adam, a local city inspector who talks about the role of the city in the remodeling process, and of course, Haege. Display tables staffed with Fairway carpenters and designers give attendees the opportunity to learn more about the company. Immediate follow up capitalized on the interest.

TEACH AN ADULT EDUCATION COURSE

Remodelers across the country encounter quality prospects while they're teaching adult education courses sponsored by their community colleges or other local organizations. Some programs are technical—like framing or masonry. Others are more general—like "How to Plan a Remodeling Project," or "Working with a Design/Build Remodeler."

Homeowners who attend these classes are excellent prospects. Few consumers understand the complexity inherent in a remodeling project. When they find out, they hire a professional to handle it! You'll be in the catbird seat. Of course, you have to be organized and knowledgeable in all of the classes you teach. The pay is usually small or non-existent, but the exposure is great. Call your local college and ask about openings in the adult education schedule. Once you've made arrangements to teach a course, send notices to your Circle of Influence and send out press releases to the community.

CHARITABLE EVENTS: MARKETING FROM THE HEART

You can reach some excellent target market prospects by participating in charitable events. This shows your preferred audience that you're not just a "taker" but are willing to give back to the people and community that support your company. If your target market is highly affluent homeowners, you may choose to donate time, materials, or cash to organizations that are favorites of the well-to-do. Schools and clubs often use auctions as fundraisers. Consider donating "A Carpenter For a Day" to the auction. Industry associations also organize charitable events.

Whenever you donate to a charitable event, be sure to mention it in communications with your previous customers. Let them know that you support organizations in which they have an interest.

 **STREET**SMARTS

When most people think of remodeling, they don't immediately think of golf. But that's exactly what sets Lee Kimball Kitchens, Inc., in Boston apart from the competition. The company created a separate non-profit entity, the David K. Johnson Foundation, to honor the company owners' father and to raise money for other organizations.

In the summer of 2003, Lee Kimball Kitchens held its third annual David K. Johnson Golf Tournament, which drew 140 golfers, more than 50 sponsors, and raised more than $12,000 to benefit the local chapter of the Alzheimer's Association and Sanborn Home Care.

Company co-owners Bruce and Gregg Johnson invited suppliers, employees, subcontractors, business associates, personal friends, and the community-at-large to participate in the golf outing. Bruce and Gregg's father, David Johnson, has progressive dementia, and the tournament enabled Lee Kimball Kitchens to give back to those who helped the family with the challenge.

"It was a great success, and we raised a lot of money," said Bruce, noting the event also provided good publicity for Lee Kimball Kitchens. "We are using the company as a vehicle to market the golf tournament. It gained exposure for the company and was picked up by the local press."

Here are Bruce's recommendations for how to set up a charitable event:

▶ Find a cause you are passionate about. Charitable events require a substantial time commitment and some financial backing, especially when you get started. Because of the learning curve, Bruce found that the first golf tournament was the hardest to organize. Now the brothers delegate more of the organizational work and spend their time on marketing and networking to draw more participation.

- Define your mission and key values. For the Johnsons, it was "To promote awareness and support for individuals and families affected by Alzheimer's disease and other progressive dementia."

  They also wanted to incorporate the "life lessons" they had learned from their parents:

  > To help and support others
  >
  > To recognize that love, support, and faith are the foundation of family
  >
  > To include having fun as part of every endeavor.

- Obtain your non-profit status from the IRS. The Johnsons had an accountant who knew how to apply for non-profit status from the IRS and who did much of the legwork for them. He warned the brothers that the application almost never goes through without having to answer additional questions and resubmit the application. The approval process took nine months, but they moved ahead with their first event during that time.

- Decide how you want to raise funds. Gregg and Bruce felt the golf tourney would deliver fun and funds and fit their potential contributor constituency. However, they may add or change their fundraiser(s) in the future. They are committed long-term to the foundation and the golf tournament is their current vehicle. Bruce recommends focusing on one type of fundraising until you master it.

- Develop a database of contacts. The Johnsons included their business contacts, personal friends, and their parents' contacts and friends. Sanborn Home Care added its database and a colleague's company, Jack's Custom Woodworking, also was willing to market the tournament to its database. The Johnsons amassed about 500 names and sold out their first tournament in 2001.

- Set up a governing committee. The Johnsons have 12 volunteers on their committee who meet monthly from March to August. Make meetings fun to attend by changing the site, planning special outings, and providing good fellowship and food. The committee helps spread out the work of organizing a charitable event and contributes contacts and brainpower along the way.

- Be prepared for company involvement and expense. The Johnsons absorb many costs, including staff time, to make the event a success. They recommend appointing a willing employee as the point person for communication and organization. They absorb the cost of event work done during the company's working hours.

YOUR WEB SITE: CREATING AN ON-LINE PRESENCE

Every professional remodeler should have a web site. Consumers are using the Internet in droves to find information about many things—including learning more about remodeling companies they are considering.

Remodelers use their web sites as company brochures that are available 24/7 to consumers. They also receive leads directly from their sites.

Pam Stanmire, president of Astro E-Design Solutions, Inc., a creative web design firm in Ellicott City, Md., (*www.design-integrity.net*), shares her must-do's for a successful web site:

- **Secure a domain name.** A domain name is the name of your web site. It's also called a URL which means Uniform Resource Locator. For example, our domain name (URL) is *www.RemodelersAdvantage.com*.

You must register a domain name to secure it for your company's exclusive use. Don't be tempted to go with an unknown company just because it's less expensive. What saves you a few bucks today may result in major problems down the road.

When developing your domain name, remember to keep it short and simple. It should be easy to remember and easy for a user to type into a browser. Do your best to incorporate the name of your company into your domain name.

Some popular resources for registering your web site URL are:
www.eNom.com
www.domain.com
www.networksolutions.com
www.register.com

> **Find a reliable, professional hosting company.** Choosing a company that offers low-cost or free hosting but forces the viewers to sit through endless pop-up ads will annoy your clients and prospects. It also makes your company look unprofessional.

> **Hire a professional to build your site.** Just like graphic design, web site design is a specific discipline. Don't be tempted to cut corners and build your own site or hire an inexperienced high school student to save money. You only have one chance to make a first impression with a visitor online. Put your best foot forward and take the time to find a professional, experienced web developer who has a balance of marketing and technical skills.

Check a potential developer's references thoroughly. (Be certain you are speaking with real businesses that the developer has actually built sites for and not the person's friends, relatives etc.) Also check with your local Better Business Bureau to research complaints against the developer.

- **Plan for a well-organized site with simple navigation.** The key to success ultimately hinges on visitors' ability to readily find information on your site. The site's navigational elements should remain consistent from page to page. Each page should have a clear way to get back "Home" and also an obvious way to find your contact information. Every company, no matter how small, should always have a "Contact" page.

- **Place a simple contact form on the "Contact" page.** Someone with insomnia may be surfing at an odd hour and will readily fill out a form at 4 a.m. but may not even remember your company's name during waking hours.

- **Use pithy content.** The site pages and corresponding content should be grouped in a logical manner that is intuitive for visitors to browse. An outside designer can be very helpful here, because it's often difficult for people inside the company to determine how information should be organized for outside viewers. How you see things from within your business may not necessarily reflect the information your customer needs to make a decision or request additional information.

  Review your company's printed materials to help you organize your site's content. Remember, your web site is really no more than an online brochure. Organize your site the way your printed materials are organized.

- **KIS (Keep it Simple).** You only have a few seconds to grab your visitors' attention and present your message. To do this, describe your business in detail and hit the key points but don't overwhelm the visitor with minutia. Keep pages to no more than a few well-written, concise paragraphs.

Many companies new to the web often try to razzle-dazzle visitors with their sites. They squander a lot of time, money, and effort on bells and whistles that do nothing for the site's effectiveness—and sometimes make it slow and difficult to access.

Instead, focus on creating a get a well-structured, easy-to-navigate, informational site. Don't spend time "over thinking" the project. You don't need the latest technology to impress visitors. People come to your site looking for one thing and one thing only: information. Give it to them in a straightforward, easy-to-access manner and your site will yield results.

PROMOTING YOUR SITE

The saying, "If you build it, they will come" is not true for web sites. Without promotion, your site will just sit on a server somewhere and never be seen by human eyes. If you want traffic, you have to make it happen. It will not happen on its own.

The most obvious way to promote your site is to put your domain name on everything: business cards, printed brochures, vehicle signage, print ads, office signage, and job site signs.

STREET SMARTS

Larry Parrish, president of Parrish Construction, Inc., in Boulder, Colo., knows his web site (*www.Parrishbuilt.com*) is an integral part of his marketing campaign. "It's indispensable, as it serves so many purposes," he says. "If we meet with one partner [of a client couple] during a sales meeting, the other person can review our credentials and systems on our site at a later time. We ask all prospective clients to review it before our first meeting so that they can learn something about us, read an article I've written, review our list of clients, and maybe even recognize a name of a friend or relative on that list."

◀ *All of the Parrish Construction vehicles feature the company's web site domain name.*

In addition, homeowners search the Internet and find the Parrish web site. "The first week our web site was up and running, we received a call from a homeowner currently living in Chicago who was moving to Boulder. He had reviewed our web site and told us over the phone that we were hired. It was a $300,000 project!"

Larry used an Internet consultant to ensure that Parrish's site is easily found by search engines and Internet businesses that search various web sites and sort them according to specific criteria. Google.com is one example of a popular search engine. Parrish's site currently receives more than 6,000 hits a week.

■ ■ ■

Be sure to submit your domain name to search engines and directories, but be prepared to wait. It may take several months to be indexed by search engines.

Search engines are quite complicated and have changed radically over the years. Optimizing and promoting your site so it ranks on a search engine can get quite pricey. While it was once simple to achieve top rankings for just about any site, it is almost impossible to rank at all today without allocating at least a small monthly budget for search engine rankings.

STREETSMARTS

Many remodeling companies find it helpful to use one of the online business directories. www.YellowPages.com is one such Internet directory. It is independently owned and receives millions of hits a week. It acts as an online Yellow Pages directory and offers businesses several ways to be listed.

Most listings consist of a simple company name and phone number as a courtesy for free. Businesses that want a stronger presence in the online Yellow Pages can purchase a listing for $500 to $800 a year (the price depends on the local population density).

This paid listing includes a color version of your company's logo, a company description of up to 128 characters, and a live link to your web site. For yet an additional investment, you can purchase a listing that covers a wider geographical range.

When someone uses an online business directory to search for a company in your niche, all company names in that category appear—but those with paid listings appear first.

Before purchasing a listing from any internet directory, do plenty of research to make sure that it will work for your company. Contact people from companies who have purchased listings and ask them about the results they've received.

■ ■ ■

FINDING A DESIGNER

Start by asking suppliers, vendors, distributors, and other business associates who did their web sites and if they are satisfied with the results and service.

Avoid falling into the common trap of "My grandson (nephew, neighbor) knows how to do web sites." Unless the person that you are being referred to is a full-time, qualified web professional, steer clear. You want a company or individual who works on web sites for a living and not as a hobby or side job.

The best place to start looking is online. A simple search for "(Your city or state) web design" should yield an abundant number of options.

Once you have pulled up some search results, start investigating. Look at each web developer's site carefully. Does it look like a professional put it together? Can you navigate the site easily? Is there any outdated information on the site? Are there any broken links? Is the spelling and grammar top-notch? Are there example sites in the online portfolio that are comparable to what you need for your site?

After you've found a professional-looking, up-to-date web designer's site and have determined that the web developer works on sites like the one you need built, contact the developer and tell him or her what you need. Be honest about what you need and what you can afford. Listen carefully to the web developer's ideas for your site. Be sure that any work the developer proposes doing will satisfy your site's requirements. For example, if all you need is a basic, informational site, don't get sold on extra features that can always be built in at a later date, such as "client login."

Check references thoroughly. Ask the developer to provide you with at least five former clients' names he or she has done work for recently. Verify that these are actual businesses and not friends or relatives of the developer. Any established developer who is on the level will have no problem providing clients' contact information. Contact these references and ask them detailed questions about the work the developer did for them. Was the project completed on time and within budget? Were they happy with the finished product? Was the developer easy to work with? What snags, if any, did they encounter during the project? Would they work with the developer again?

As with any other profession, web developers charge a wide range of fees. Don't be tempted to hire a company simply because it's the most affordable. Take all factors into consideration when evaluating a potential company to build your site. Here are some things to consider:

- Is this a company you feel comfortable talking to?
- Does the company promptly return phone calls and e-mails?
- Does this company have stellar references and a good history of satisfied clients?
- Do you like the designs the company has done for other clients?
- Most importantly, does the company understand your needs?

Once you've selected a web development company to work with, make sure you have a detailed agreement with your developer that outlines the specifics of what you are getting, exactly how much it will cost, a payment schedule, and what happens if a dispute arises. If the web developer balks at providing such specifics, walk away. A professional web developer will want to ensure that you have all of that information in writing before starting a project.

Stanmire says, "Make sure you receive a copy of your site on CD-ROM. This is imperative. If the server hosting your site loses data during a disaster, you could potentially lose your entire site unless you have a backup copy. Don't rely on your host to maintain a backup. I've seen many businesses lose their entire sites because they did not have backup copies of them."

HOW OFTEN SHOULD YOU UPDATE YOUR SITE?

Plan on adding fresh content at least twice a year. These can be simple changes such as adding new photos or updating sales information. It may take visitors some time to decide to go forward with a project and in the process, they may visit your site several times. That's why it's best to keep content fresh and remove outdated info from your site.

As for a site overhaul, plan on a fresh new "look" for a site about every two years. As web technology continues to evolve and trends change, visitors can easily identify sites that haven't been revamped in a few years.

Until recently, business owners had to invest in expensive web editing programs and master technical skills such as HTML and FTP to update their web sites.

That has all changed thanks to the use of inexpensive content management systems (CMS). Discuss CMS with your web developer to find out if it's realistic for someone in your office who has the time and the enthusiasm to learn a new task to regularly update your web site. A good web developer can help you find an affordable, easy-to-use CMS that gives you more control over your web site.

The best CMS systems are browser-based web site management applications. You simply open up a browser and log into a password-protected area on your server. Once you've logged in you can easily edit and update your web site. You don't need programming knowledge or skills. If you can use Microsoft Word, you can use a simple content management system. This software is a great investment if you plan to make frequent changes to your site.

PROSPECT MARKETING PLAN AND BUDGET

Your Circle of Influence is your most important lead generating resource. Prospect marketing is second in importance, so create a strong program here as well. In fact, many remodelers need only these two areas to provide all the leads they can use in a year.

Below, create a list of the tactics you feel would work best for your company in your market. Then determine the dollar investment each tactic would require to develop an overall budget for this segment.

 TACTICS/EFFORTS COST

Job site signs	$ _____
Job site mailings	$ _____
Canvassing	$ _____
Networking	$ _____
Telemarketing	$ _____
Open house	$ _____
Remodeled home tour	$ _____
Special events	$ _____
Educational seminar	$ _____
Adult education class	$ _____
Charitable events	$ _____
Web site	$ _____
Other _____	$ _____
_____	$ _____
TOTAL BUDGET	$ _____

part five

BUILD A FLOW OF NEW BUYERS WITH YOUR UNIVERSE MARKETING PROGRAM

Exploring Media Advertising

Home and Mall Shows:
A Lead Generation Opportunity

Winning Awards: Making Your Projects Shine

Generating Publicity: Spotlight Your Company

Maximizing Visibility with a Showroom

Yellow Pages: How Much Should You Spend?

Hosting a Radio Talk Show

Using Co-op Advertising

Universe Marketing Plan and Budget

Marketing to your universe means targeting your entire market area, whether the people are qualified prospects or not. These tactics reach a large number of people who aren't candidates for your products or services—and can be a waste of your marketing dollars. But this can also be an effective way to reach prospective customers who hadn't heard of you before. Because you're reaching such a large number of people, these tactics tend to be the most expensive and produce the lowest quality leads.

Companies with small marketing budgets should use universe marketing tactics only after they've implemented the other more effective methods of marketing discussed previously. However, companies requiring a larger number of leads to reach their sales volume goals may need to reach out to the entire area.

There are many ways to reach this broad market—everything from hot-air balloons, full-color catalog mailings, and home shows to advertising on local television. In this section, we will outline the most popular and effective universe marketing methods.

EXPLORING MEDIA ADVERTISING

Media advertising includes all print ads (newspapers, magazines, billboards) or broadcast commercials (network or cable television, radio). These media tactics can be expensive, so do careful research before investing large amounts of money.

NEWSPAPER ADVERTISING

Newspapers reach hundreds of thousands of readers each day and can be a prime spot in which to place your message. Because newspapers are printed daily or weekly, their material is very timely, allowing you to quickly reach your audience with specials, sales, or announcements. Your message can reach a very large audience for only a few pennies per person. In addition to the large, metropolitan newspaper in your city, dozens of smaller newspapers target select markets and can be a much better marketing investment for your company. A recent survey done by the Newspaper Association of America found that 70% of owners of homes valued at $250,000 or more read daily newspapers, and that 77% of this population read Sunday editions.

If you're considering newspaper advertising, carefully review each publication's target readers. Information on demographics, specifications, distribution quantities, and locations may be found on the newspaper's web site—a great place to start your research. Be sure to answer these questions:

1. Do the readers match the demographics of the market I'm trying to attract?

2. Are the newspapers distributed in the geographic areas I'd like to reach? Major newspapers may offer regional "runs" in which your ad is placed only in those papers delivered in a certain geographic area.

Next, design an ad campaign that will produce leads. Here are some tips for creating a print advertising campaign that works:

▸ Consistency, frequency and patience are the keys to a successful campaign. Plan to run your ad many times before you expect it to generate results. Unless you're running a special offer such as a sale, most people will probably need several exposures to your message before they act. According to the Newspaper Association of America, your audience needs to be exposed to your ad 2.5 times before it sinks in and they begin to build awareness and familiarity with your company.

▸ Your ad campaign is not just for flush times. During the Great Depression and the two World Wars, many companies continued to run their ads even though many people had no money to spend. But once people were able to spend money again, they chose the brands they remembered seeing in advertisements.

▸ When you prepare your ad, concentrate on creating strong, eye-catching headlines. For many readers, the headline is the only line worth reading. Make certain your headline and artwork or photography work well together.

▸ Include a strong "call-to-action" in your ad. Tell your prospects what you'd like them to do after reading your ad: visit your showroom, call for a free design consultation, call for a free informational brochure. What do you want them to do?

▸ Try to be consistent with your ad sizes, templates, type styles, formats, the day you run the ad, and your brand. In fact, keep production costs low by creating only one or two ads that will run again and again. Studies show that a single ad can be used effectively for up to nine months without a reduction in response.

▸ Include white space. Crammed ads get poor results because readers don't want to work that hard to read them.

▸ Mention the benefit to the reader. Prospective customers want to know "what's in it for me." However, don't try to pack the ad with reasons to buy—give the customers one primary reason, and then back it up with one or two secondary reasons.

MAGAZINE ADVERTISING

Magazines are another way to reach a broad market base. As with all media, there are pros and cons in magazine advertising.

Pros

▸ Magazines are beautiful and because of the quality of the publication, photography can really shine.

- Magazine subscribers tend to be very loyal readers a up a magazine several times over the course of a month.

- Magazines have a long shelf-life—they're not thrown away for at least a few weeks.

Cons

- Because magazines typically come out only once a month, it's difficult to promote sales or other specials that run for a short time. Therefore, companies tend to use "institutional" ads. These can be good for creating an image for the company over the long term, but less effective in generating solid leads immediately.

- Magazine lead time is extensive. Your ad must be delivered up to six weeks before it will appear. This means that you're stuck if your needs change.

- The costs can be prohibitive.

Before spending money on a magazine advertisement, check the demographics of the publication's readers to make sure that they match those of your best prospects. This can be an expensive tactic for most remodeling companies.

RADIO ADVERTISING

Radio is a relatively inexpensive ad medium. Ninety-nine percent of American homes have radios and approximately 50 million new radios are sold each year. But the advertiser has only sound to work with, so the message is fleeting. Prime time includes morning and evening drive time, when audiences are the largest and advertising is the most expensive. Commercials are sold in 10-, 30-, and 60- second spots and are packaged with specific placement times and frequency.

Radio listeners are loyal to a particular station. Each station's content is carefully targeted to a particular audience demographic.

Many stations focus on very narrow bands of listeners, such as specific ethnic groups, business professionals, teens, or older listeners. When you're choosing a radio station, pick the one with demographics that are closest to your prime customers'. This probably means homeowners in the 30-to-65 year-old age group.

To find out which station might be your best choice for radio advertising, ask your customers what station they listen to. Conduct your own basic sampling. Ask the station's sales representative to supply you with a media kit, which will tell you how many listeners the radio station attracts, who they are, and when they listen.

Radio time is worthless if it's not sold, so stations often will give you volume discounts and additional time instead of reducing the cost of your ad. High-volume advertising periods are October, November, and December because of the holidays. These months are most appealing to retail stores and are not as effective for remodelers.

Radio commercials are often produced by the radio station. If you have a package contract with them, they may throw in the production at no cost. Negotiate for better time slots or free ad production. Contact ad agencies and audio-visual firms that also produce radio ads. Three common formats are the "donut" ad, the testimonial, and the live announcer. Select the most appropriate format for your listening audience:

▸ In the **donut**, the beginning and end of the ads stay the same; anytime a new ad is needed, you simply replace the central message.

▸ In **testimonials**, the announcer interviews a previous client and questions him or her about your company's performance. The client's glowing, sincere reports can create a very effective advertising campaign.

- When the **"live"** announcer acts as your company spokesperson, you'll get some of your most creative commercials—although you won't know what to expect. Announcers work from a script, but they also have the opportunity to ad lib. To get the most from announcers, take them on a tour of your jobs to give them an idea of the type of work you do. This will give them the background they need to make your commercial special.

The effectiveness of radio advertising directly relates to the frequency with which the ad is heard. Research shows that it's most successful to run a campaign of ads and concentrate them over a two- to four-week schedule. Sometimes remodelers will run ads for two weeks, and then no ads for two weeks. Consumers get the impression that the ads are still running during that down period.

Radio is an ad medium that works best in combination with other tactics. It's a reinforcer. Plan on working with radio ads for about six months until you figure out the best way to use this medium for your company.

A key to developing the right radio advertisement is to keep it simple. One pro likened it to a "poster for the ears"—there's only room for one message.

▼

Matt Mills, general sales manager of WTOP, an all-news station in Washington, D.C., has been helping businesses use radio effectively for 12 years. He says, "The remodeling business has one advantage that some other businesses don't have when it comes to radio—the ability to use 'theater of the mind' to generate interest in the product." Mills describes theater of the mind as the ability to portray the product in such a compelling way that the listener visualizes the product clearly and imagines him or herself using it.

"Apply that concept to remodeling," Mills explains. "With a visual advertisement, you are showing someone a house that has been remodeled and while that can be effective, it can also cause folks to say 'that doesn't look like my house', 'my house isn't that big,' 'I couldn't afford that,' etc.

"With radio, the advertisement gets the listener to think about how cramped their kitchen is, how the sink isn't in the correct location, how the floor is dingy and needs some work, etc. With this commercial, the listener pictures *their* house and they get excited about the possibility of remodeling."

Mills adds, "In order to make any advertising effective, someone needs to be exposed to the advertisement an average of three times before they respond to it.

"Don't run advertising over the entire year. Spend more over a shorter time period rather than less over a longer time period. Don't get caught up in thinking you need to have a 'presence.' Assuming the commercial is written effectively, you will get much farther with a more intensive, high-frequency campaign over a shorter period of time.

"When creating your commercial, focus on using 'theater of the mind' to generate excitement, and be sure to answer the following questions: 'Why buy from me?' This sets you apart from your competitors. 'Why buy now?' provides a call to action."

TELEVISION ADVERTISING

Advertising on television is the form of advertising that's most like personal selling. You're in the consumer's home and they can see and hear your ad. With good television advertising, viewers may perceive your remodeling company as a nationally recognized name. Communicating to prospective customers via television can be particularly effective because of the medium's ability to convey emotion and feeling through the use of video, sound, and color.

In the past, only the largest remodeling companies used television advertising because it was very expensive. But, with the abundance of television stations and networks offering advertising at attractive rates, TV ads are becoming more popular for companies of all sizes.

As with other advertising mediums, television advertising allows you to target specific audiences according to the demographics that a particular show or network serves. With targeted ad placement, you can reach a largely female audience by running TV ads during the day, reach men by running ads during sporting events, target children with ads during children's shows, or professionals with ads run during the evening news.

You can also target homeowners who are specifically interested in remodeling by running ads in conjunction with the dozens of home and garden programs that are so popular. In fact, these home improvement shows are so popular there is now an entire network dedicated to this programming.

Prime time is evening, when the largest audience is watching. And Americans do watch their televisions—an estimated six hours a day. The average viewer is bombarded with up to 20,000 commercials a year!

Unlike radio advertising, television commercials must be professionally produced by a TV station or an ad agency. In addition, you'll be charged for the production of a TV ad.

CABLE TELEVISION ADVERTISING

More and more small businesses use cable television advertising as a broadcast option for their marketing messages.

Chris Broulline, sales manager of Comcast Television of Montgomery County, Md., says there are three keys to success for using this medium:

"First, pick the right networks. While some networks like Home & Garden Television (HGTV) are a natural for remodeling companies, some others would be great but not quite so obvious. Networks such as the Food Network may attract the kinds of people who want, and can afford, home remodeling.

"Second, have enough frequency to make it work. When using national advertising, companies look for reach—how many households their ad will reach. Not so with cable. Here, you choose the audience you want, even if it's small, and hit them often enough to entice them to take action. If you can only run one or two spots, save your money.

"Third, do the right things with your creative output. You have to create a compelling message with a strong call to action. Your local cable station will help you produce your commercial, using their extensive experience in what works and what doesn't on cable television."

One of the benefits of advertising on cable is the ability to select specific territories in which your commercial will air. Remodeling companies can purchase commercials in three ways:

- National, which includes the entire network.
- Regional, which includes all the homes in a metro area.
- Local, which allows you to pick specific areas for your commercial to air.

The investment for advertising on cable TV can range from several hundred to several thousand dollars. Costs depend on the number of households the network reaches, the ratings the particular show has earned, and the supply and demand for a particular network. "A great demand for a network will drive prices up," Chris Broulline says. "For example, the Golf Network doesn't reach many households but companies know that the people who watch golf tend to have money and be highly educated. So they want to buy space on that network. This demand has driven prices up over what the ratings would normally demand."

The sales representative at your local cable company will be able to help you sort through the various options and determine if cable television advertising is something you should add to your marketing plan.

HOME AND MALL SHOWS: A LEAD GENERATION OPPORTUNITY

Home and mall shows can be outstanding opportunities to meet and talk to hundreds or even thousands of potential buyers. These shows differ from each other. Home show visitors pay money to spend some time looking and thinking about purchases related to the home. They're focused on the same theme as the exhibitors.

Mall show visitors happen upon the show while they visit the mall for other purposes. Because they're not as focused, mall show leads are generally of lesser quality than home show leads.

Before participating in any show, do your research. If possible, visit the show before you decide to sign up. That way you can scope out how the show is doing and how it will do for you. Want to determine which shows will work best for you?

Here are some factors to consider:

- How well is the show promoted? Are most local homeowners going to hear about it? Is it scheduled for a time of year when you'll need leads? Does it conflict with a holiday or an important sporting event?

- Get demographic information from the show organizers. How many people attend? Is any information available about attendee ages, homeownership, or income levels? If so, see how those characteristics match your prime customers'.

- How does the show look to you? Is it lively? Are there good crowds? Have exhibitors spent time, money, and effort on good looking booths? What is the mix of exhibitors? Are your competitors there? The presence of other companies like yours may signal a good marketing tactic. On the other hand, an absence of competitive companies may mean that you'll have a wide-open playing field and it may be worth a one-year test.

- Visit on the last day of the show and interview some of the exhibitors to learn about what kind of results they've received from participating in the show. Have they received lots of good leads?

- Review the booth designs for ideas on what works and what doesn't.

- Analyze traffic patterns to determine where the prime booth space is located. Where would you want to locate your booth if you decide to participate?

Answering these questions will give you a good idea of whether or not you should invest in home or mall shows. As a marketing tactic, it's not inexpensive.

Before making any decision, consider the sum of these costs:

- Staffing
- Booth space and labor to build
- Company display materials
- Give-aways

Staffing is one of the most costly aspects of participating in shows. To get the most out of a show, your booth must be manned at all times. This may mean 10:00 am to 10:00 pm in some cases. These long days will require two or more shifts of knowledgeable employees. If you have plenty of salespeople, this may not be too difficult. However, if you have a one- or two-person company, plan on working long, hard hours while the show is open.

 STREETSMARTS

Kent Eberle, president of Eberle Remodeling, Inc., in Sacramento, Calif, participates in two home shows each year and feels that the investment is well worth it. "Our main goal at the show is exposure," he says, "Being at the show for many years demonstrates to clients that you are here to stay and are a legitimate company to deal with."

To maximize the results, Kent sends out two letters after the shows to prospects who filled out information request forms while attending the shows. Spaced a week apart, the letters encourage the prospects to contact Eberle again, help disqualify the tire kickers, and allow the company to quickly get in touch with prospects who are serious buyers.

Are home shows hard work? "You bet!" says Kent. "You'll have sore feet, a weary back, and you'll become very tired of talking to people. But you'll also be in front of thousands of people right in your market."

One of the shows in which Eberle Remodeling participates attracted over 50,000 people.

And it paid off. In 2003 alone, the company attracted over $300,000 in new business directly attributable to the home show.

■ ■ ■

Booth Space

Space is usually sold in square-foot units—10'x10' is a common booth size. The size increases in 10' increments—10'x 20', 10'x30', etc. Design your booth to be open and comfortable. It should invite people into the space—not block them from entering. Beautifully furnished booths are memorable. One remodeler purchased low-cost, rich-looking furniture specifically to use in his home show booth.

Company Display Materials

Many companies develop ingenious, reusable booths that considerably cut their costs over time. Read the show's rules to see whether you will be allowed to set up the booth or will need to hire expensive union show workers to do it.

Build your booth to reduce any set-up expenses detailed in the rules. Remember to plan on carpeting and padding, plants, flattering lighting, and a variety of quality photographs of your projects. When budgeting, don't forget to factor in labor costs to actually build the booth. Depending on the complexity of the design, the construction could take several days to several weeks. Build your booth in modules so it can be easily detached and hauled in and out of the showroom.

Give-Aways

These can range from company brochures or special promotion flyers to specialty items like yardsticks and magnets. Make sure prospects walk away with information including your company name, address, telephone number, and web site address.

Take the time to qualify the prospects who visit through your booth. Some remodelers consider every person who walks in the booth as a lead. However, they don't have the time or staff to follow up on all of them. If you can't follow up on qualified leads, you're wasting your investment. It's much more effective to be very selective about who you designate as a "lead" and to work only with the best leads—those people who are highly qualified.

Identify Your Home Show Goals

Remodelers participate in home and mall shows to increase public awareness of their companies and gather leads. Participation can also help you reach specific marketing goals like the ones below.

Are you trying to gather as many names as possible to add to your database for future marketing efforts?

A raffle in your booth encourages prospects to complete entry blanks, which gives you the opportunity to gather detailed information for your database. It also increases traffic to the point that you might not be able to speak to every person, so staff accordingly. To attract more qualified prospects, choose a raffle prize that appeals to people who are actively considering a remodeling project. Examples include a free remodeling feasibility study or initial design. If you don't offer a targeted prize, the raffle may generate leads of a lower quality.

Do you need immediate leads to increase your current workload?

Speak to every person who walks into your booth so that you can determine whether or not they are a good lead. Try to pull them into conversation with questions like:

> What type of remodeling project are you planning?
> Why are you remodeling?
> Where is your home located?
> When would you like to have the project completed?
> How much research have you done so far?
> Have you ever remodeled before?
> Tell me about your home.

Use a lead card to keep track of only the best leads. Rate the leads with letters (a=hot, b=possible, c=low quality) or numbers at the home show while the information is fresh in your mind. This approach allows you to immediately contact the "hot" leads once you're back in your office. Don't rely on your memory. The shortest pencil is more powerful than the longest memory.

Would you like to set appointments at the show? Have an appointment book ready in your booth. Fill in several of the appointment slots to give the impression that you're busy; people like to work with successful people. Then ask for the appointment.

INCLUDE AN EDUCATIONAL SEMINAR

Many home shows include seminar space and schedule exhibitors to present seminars. Ask if the show you're considering participating in offers consumer seminars and if you can present one or two sessions. Possible topics include, *"Ten Mistakes to Avoid When Building an Addition," "The Facts About Replacement Windows," "What Are Your Remodeling Goals?"* and *"New Trends in Kitchen Design."*

"Presenting seminars at the shows is a great way to gain increased publicity and name recognition," says Kent Eberle of Eberle Remodeling, Inc.

Have informational sheets available that include your company name, address, telephone number, web site, and your booth number. Don't sell your services. Instead, by offering valuable information, you'll establish your expertise and create demand by being up-front and knowledgeable.

HOME SHOW TRICKS OF THE TRADE

- Show crowds move at a pace of two to three miles per hour. There is about a three-second window in which people decide whether your booth is or is not worth entering. Slow them down with something eye-catching.

- The booth's first impression must speak to your prime buyer and must communicate what your prime job is. Target your buyer. If you're looking for a price buyer, make that a dominant theme. If you're targeting high-end buyers, make sure your booth draws them quickly and effectively.

- Don't have too many areas of focus in the booth. Prospects should be able to stand 20 feet away and know immediately who you are and what you sell.

- A bright company banner hung from the ceiling can be very effective and can be seen from across the hall.

- Booth craftsmanship is critical. Potential buyers check out your booth for clues about the quality of your company's work. Don't turn them off with poor construction.

- Suppliers often make their displays available to their customers. Check your suppliers for beautiful, free components that can dress up your booth nicely.

- Entry and exit areas should be kept open. Show attendees avoid booths with narrow openings and exits. Design your booth with an open floor plan.

- Activities will draw prospects into your booth. Popcorn or candy also attracts people, but your true prospects may be missed. Contests are popular, but if you do one make sure it's related to your company niche. A "Carpenter for the Day" is a popular prize and gives your company an opportunity to show off your work for a prospective client.

- At least half of all literature that showgoers collect gets thrown out at shows; it never even makes it out the door. Because you need some type of literature to hand out to prospects, produce an inexpensive piece you'll be able to hand out freely. If it's expensive or in limited supply, give it only to people who you've identified as quality prospects.

- Send a letter to your Circle of Influence list inviting them to the show. Offer free or discounted tickets if possible.

- Incorporate enlarged "before" and "after" photos into your display—showgoers love them! Show photos of the types of jobs that you want to do.

- Don't put chairs in the booth. Staff should never sit down—they won't get back up readily and showgoers will use the chairs to rest. Drafting-height stools let employees perch, rest, and still look active.

Home and mall shows bring in hundreds of people who will see your booth and remember your company name. It's a great way to have face-to-face contact with prospects in your market.

WINNING AWARDS:
MAKING YOUR PROJECTS SHINE

Winning an award is an excellent way to demonstrate that you are a top-quality remodeler. It's a form of third-party endorsement—your peers, an association, or a publication tell the world that they think your company is very special. The award is an affirmation of the efforts you're putting into your company. It's also an opportunity to blow your own horn a bit and raise your company's status in the eyes of your customers, prospects, employees, subs, and suppliers.

The quest for an award is a learning experience. It is unusual to win on the first attempt. Instead, remodelers create the best entry they can, send it off, notice who wins, and take every opportunity to examine the entries and winning jobs.

You'll win an award when your entry accomplishes two things—you have a perfectly wonderful project that is well decorated or landscaped by the homeowner, and your entry tells a superb story. Luck and the right homeowner provide the first part of that equation. We can help you with the second part. Here are some tips to position yourself for the best chance to win an award:

‣ Watch industry publications and association mailings for notices about upcoming award competitions.

‣ Read contest rules thoroughly and follow them to the letter. Don't take the chance of being disqualified due to a technicality.

‣ Create a concise, well-organized presentation book. Decide how to tell your story. The entry should include top-quality photos and written descriptions.

‣ Use "before" photos whenever possible to demonstrate the radical improvements your work created. Try to take the "befores" from the same angles as the "after" photos. "During" photos are also interesting additions to your presentation.

- Hire a professional photographer for "after" shots. A professional's skills—especially lighting—can make your project look fantastic instead of only attractive. Be on site during the photo shoot so you can help clean up and clear away toys or garden tools.

- Ask the photographer to shoot both color and black-and-white photos. Color photos do not always convert easily to high-quality black-and-white shots, which is the preferred format for newspapers.

- "Before" and "after" floor plans provide an important perspective. Consider transparent overlays to show the changes.

- Add captions to all photos. Make your narrative descriptive.

- Use a "Problem/Solution" format. Talk about why the customer wanted to remodel in the first place (problem) and then describe how your company helped develop the right solution.

- Emphasize an angle in the story to help sell it to the judges. Is the project a historic structure? Does it include a particularly interesting technical problem? Is there a human interest angle?

- If the contest doesn't provide binders and formats for entries, make your presentation creative. Use colored construction paper to frame photos. Put each page in a plastic cover. Desktop publishing software can produce professional quality text.

- Write as you would for an interested layperson. While contests are run by professional associations and industry publications, the judging may be done by people who may not be familiar with highly detailed blueprints or technical jargon.

STREETSMARTS

Anthony Wilder Design/Build, Inc., in Bethesda, Md., has won more than 100 project awards since the company's inception. President Liz Wilder says, "When entering a contest, be sure to specifically answer the questions that are asked. For example, one contest asks what innovative products were used in the project. Don't gloss this over. Answer it explicitly. Sometimes judges don't have extensive technical expertise, so you have to really spell it out.

"Next, let the photos tell the story. Use as few words as you can and let the visuals carry the message. And it goes without saying that you should always use high-quality, professional photography."

After you win an award, send copies of the entry to newspapers and magazines to give them an overview of the project. "The writer can view the entry and decide if it's right for their publication without a lot of involvement from us or from the homeowner," says Liz.

By doing double duty, the award entry easily pays for itself.

■ ■ ■

If you win an award, let everyone know. Your staff comes first. Send out a memo or personally tell every person on your staff. Have a party to celebrate! Let them know that you're proud of your team. Then, immediately send an announcement out to your Circle of Influence.

Then tell the media about your award. In the next section we'll discuss a variety of methods for getting your exciting news in print.

GENERATING PUBLICITY: SPOTLIGHT YOUR COMPANY

Publicity is the art of getting your name or your company's name in the media. It's one of the most valuable forms of marketing because it provides a highly credible, third-party testimonial about the quality of your company. And it's easier than you think.

The first step in generating publicity is to create a database of media contacts at newspapers (especially the smaller, local publications), industry publications, magazines, and association publications. Find this information at your local library. In the Washington, D.C., area the United Fund publishes a *Media Factbook* that includes addresses, contacts, and deadlines for every television station, radio station, newspaper, and magazine in that metropolitan area. Check your community for a similar publication.

The second step in generating publicity is to think of newsworthy topics to address in your press releases. Be creative. Many activities that you think are mundane actually have news value. Everyone in your media database should receive at least four to six press releases about you and/or your company each year.

While you don't "pay" for publicity outright like you do advertising, it can pay to invest in a professional public relations specialist who knows the local media, has a track record of article placements for his/her client, and can help you reach specific goals. To find this superstar, check the Public Relations Society of America's web site (*www.prsa.org*) for members in your area. Or call a local editor of your newspaper's home or real estate sections to ask which public relations professional they like working with. Small agencies or individual public relations agents are typically the most effective for small businesses with limited funds.

Cary Griffin, president of the marketing communications firm Griffin & Company *(www.griffinco.com)* in Washington, D.C., suggests that remodelers think about exactly what they'd like to accomplish in the next year before doing interviews. For example, do you want to be featured once or twice in the home section of a major area newspaper? Do you want to be a regular resource for editors writing stories about the remodeling industry? Would you like a spread in a glossy magazine? Or would you simply like to regularly feature company announcements like new employees or awards you've won in the business section?

What benefits do you hope to gain from working with a public relations professional? A goal of "greater awareness in the marketplace" is very difficult to measure without costly market research. The more specific your publicity goals, the better you can judge the results. "After you set your expectations, be sure to budget enough money to get the results you want," Cary adds. "Your public relations firm can help you determine the right budget to get the job done."

Here are some possible topics for press releases. Let everyone know that you've:

- Attended a national convention (Headline idea: "Local Remodeler Attends National Industry Convention")
- Taught a class on remodeling
- Been featured in a national magazine (Headline idea: "Local Remodeler Featured in National Publication")
- Earned an industry designation
- Won an award
- Attended an educational seminar
- Written an article for a trade publication
- Donated time or materials to a local charity

- Had an office open house
- Celebrated a company anniversary
- Begun to carry a new product line
- Hired a new employee
- Sent your employees to an educational seminar
- Incorporated new building techniques into your work
- Sponsored a high school contest
- Conducted a homeowner survey on remodeling trends

Any of these activities are enough to generate several articles in your local press. But if you're stumped, call several newspapers and ask for their editorial calendar. This will tell you which special topics they'll feature in a particular issue. Most newspapers have special Home Improvement issues in the spring and fall.

STREETSMARTS

◄

Bill Simone, president of Custom Design & Construction, in Los Angeles, Calif., has been featured in dozens of publications including, *The Los Angeles Times, The San Jose Mercury News, Time Magazine, Smart Money Magazine* and others.

"Much of our coverage has come from the large amount of time that I volunteer to the industry," Bill says. As president of the local Remodelors Council and vice president of the Building Industry Association (BIA)—Southern California Los Angeles East Chapter, he's in the catbird seat when the media come looking for an expert in the remodeling industry.

One of Bill's employee's supplements this publicity by sending an array of press releases to all major media outlets, including the local radio stations. It all adds up to a significant presence in the local press.

■ ■ ■

Don't be discouraged if the large, metropolitan daily newspapers don't run your releases. They're besieged with press releases from hundreds of companies. Instead, concentrate on the smaller, local publications that are always looking for filler articles.

STREET SMARTS

Mike Steed, co-owner of Steed Remodeling in Kansas City, Mo., decided to take the plunge and invest in a public relations specialist to increase the company's exposure in the Kansas City market. "We'd met her at a business organization meeting and worked with her on some basic marketing consulting," Mike says. "Then we decided to use her again to get us in the press."

The public relations professional started by creating an extensive press kit that includes in-depth information about Steed Remodeling. "She interviewed us and several of our clients to get a real picture of the service we offer our customers," Mike says. "Then she sent press kits to several of the top publications in the area. After they were sent, the follow up began."

For months, the public relations pro contacted the publications and urged them to do stories on a very hot topic – remodeling. Eight months later, Mike received a call from *The Kansas City Star,* the city's main newspaper. Because of the extensive coaching he'd received from the PR firm on how to talk to the media, Mike was able to help refocus the conversation from a general article on the evolution of the remodeling industry to one that focused on Steed Remodeling's systems and services.

"We received a huge response from this article," Mike says. "Dozens of our customers who read the article contacted us with congratulations. And we sold two jobs to people who didn't realize that we were still around!"

Mike was very pleased with the response as well as the relatively small $3,000 investment.

■ ■ ■

Once an article about your company is published, cut it out and send reprints to your customer base. Include a copy of the article in your presentation book. Remember, people believe what they read. And this third party testimonial will do much for your company image.

PRESS RELEASE GUIDELINES

1. At the top of the page, put your organization's name, address, e-mail address, and the name and phone numbers (work and home) of a contact person.

2. Leave enough space in the margins so that the editor has room to edit or insert instructions.

3. Releases should be typed and double-spaced.

4. If the release runs more than one page, write "more" at the bottom of each page and put a short heading at the top of all pages except the first (e.g., "Oak Construction, page 2").

5. Begin the release with a date or the words "For Immediate Release."

Don't worry about the exact format of your press release. The newsroom is most concerned about its content, readability, and accuracy. After you've submitted your press release, be sure to call the newsroom to verify receipt. Submission guidelines and contact phone numbers can often be found on the newspaper's web site.

PUBLICITY PHOTOGRAPHS

Daily papers often send their own photographers to news events or other events related to a feature story. While most papers prefer to use their own photos, some will print a good picture that has been sent to them. There aren't any hard rules for effective pictures, but it's always best to show something happening, rather than a group of smiling people lined up looking into the camera. Be sure the contrast is good and the subjects are in sharp focus.

Here are some tips for taking and submitting publicity photos:

▸ Except for the covers of Sunday supplements, newspapers rarely use color photos. Those they do run are usually shot by staff photographers. However, ask your photographer to take both color and black-and-white photos in case you find a future use for color shots.

▸ All pictures should have captions identifying the photo, place, date and event. Write the caption material on the lower half of a sheet of paper and tape it to the back of the photo so that the caption material shows at the bottom. Again, be sure to include the contact information.

▸ Some remodelers use a photo and detail-filled caption as their entire mailing—without an actual press release—and receive outstanding results.

Sample Press Releases

FOR IMMEDIATE RELEASE

Contact: Elizabeth Peters

Work: (301) 588-8172

Home: (301) 000-0000

LOCAL REMODELER WINS NATIONAL AWARD

June 7, 2003, Silver Spring, MD—Bob Smith, president of All American Remodeling, was awarded the Superior Gold Award for Excellence in Workmanship from the National Association of Remodelers, USA. NARU President Rebecca Oliver said, "All American Remodeling is the epitome of professionalism in remodeling today. Their concern for the quality of their product, as well as their excellence in customer service, makes this company one of the best."

Bob Smith has successfully operated All American Remodeling, a full-service remodeling company located in Silver Spring, MD, since 1980. "I'm truly honored to be the recipient of this award," said Smith, "I'm delighted that our efforts to constantly improve have been noticed by our peers."

Smith, one of the state's few Certified Graduate Remodelers (CGR), has won several awards in the past for both personal and professional achievement.

FOR IMMEDIATE RELEASE

For more information:

Deborah Hunter

Work: (301) 588-8172

Home: (301) 222-2222

LOCAL REMODELER JOINS NATIONAL INDUSTRY THINK-TANK

October 9, 2003, Ann Arbor, MI—Teddy Morgan, CEO of Morgan Builders, recently attended a meeting of Remodelers Advantage Roundtables, an industry think-tank for top remodelers. Fifteen remodeling executives from across the nation met in Ann Arbor to provide each other with input and advice on how they can continually improve the services and products their companies offer.

These Roundtable participants review financials, develop organizational charts, create future profit scenarios, and create systems that will add efficiency and predictability to their companies. Lee Bart from Alexis Building Supplies, manufacturer of quality building products, participated in the October 9 program to gain in-depth information about the remodeling industry.

"I am thrilled to have this ongoing in-depth experience to draw from," says Morgan. "Since I joined Remodelers Advantage Roundtables in 1999, this group of professional remodelers has become my informal board of directors and has made a dramatic difference in the way I run my company. They've helped me pinpoint areas for improvement and give me their input on the areas in which our company is particularly strong. With this feedback, we'll be able to heighten the level of expertise and service that we offer, which helps us deliver even more value to our customers."

Remodelers Advantage Roundtables has over 150 member companies from around the country. The program, in existence since 1990, is specifically tailored for the owners of companies that have annual sales volume of more than $1,000,000. In addition to the company reviews, RAR incorporates state-of-the-art business resources to help each Roundtable member reach a higher level of success within his or her business.

Morgan Builders is a remodeling firm that specializes in high-end residential remodeling and custom home building. They have been working with area homeowners since 1992. Morgan is an active member of the Local Chapter of the National Association of the Remodeling Industry and has recently been awarded the Contractor of the Year Award. The company is located at 1997 Falcon Boulevard, Ann Arbor, MI 48107. For more information on the services it offers, call 734-555-0321.

MAXIMIZING VISIBILITY WITH A SHOWROOM

Showrooms can be very effective lead generation tools, but they require a large time and financial investment.

The minute you open a showroom, you've gone into the retail business. If you're creating a showroom to encourage walk-in traffic, you'll have to be open and staffed during regular retail hours. The person staffing the showroom must be paid even if no one walks in. Plus, he or she must be knowledgeable enough about the products and the business to answer most of the questions prospects can think up. Experts recommend budgeting $50,000 to $100,000 to create a well-designed and appointed showroom.

Some industry pros say the money you invest in building a show room will begin to pay off in profits in two to three years. They recommend that your volume approach $1,000,000 before you take on a showroom's heavy overhead.

However, if you can swing the expense, a wonderful retail location and a beautiful showroom will attract prospects to your company. In addition, if you offer the right mix of services and avoid being considered a direct competitor, you can sell your showroom as a resource to other builders or remodelers. A showroom will increase community awareness of your business and will provide a high-profile opportunity for additional marketing tactics (such as cooking classes held in your kitchen showroom).

Andrew Shore, president of Sea Pointe Construction in Irvine, Calif., says it took the company seven or eight years before it could really justify the showroom's expense. "In hindsight, we weren't taking enough expense into consideration," he says. "We needed to really increase our volume to validate the showroom." Now, with a volume of just over $4,000,000, Sea Pointe boasts a 2,100-square-foot, elegant showroom that has become a cornerstone of the company's marketing efforts.

"A well-planned showroom makes a huge difference in our ability to sell at a higher mark up," Andrew says. "It helps the client see the company as an established, permanent business. It gives them confidence in us." The Sea Pointe team uses the showroom as a giant closing room. "We do all of our proposal and contract presentations in the showroom so the prospective clients are surrounded by our work. We sell the sizzle."

Other benefits of a showroom include streamlining the often-difficult selections process. "One of our major selling points is that we make sure that all products they select coordinate and work well with each other to ensure a beautiful space. We can do that because it's all right here in front of them," Andrew says.

The showroom also gives the salesperson more control over the process. "We used to send our customers to a variety of suppliers to choose their materials," he says, "and sometimes, they wouldn't come back! Sometimes our vendors would offer to do parts of the projects for less money than we would. It was infuriating. Now, we do all selections here so it's not a problem."

Andrew's learned some hard lessons since he opened his showroom 12 years ago. He offers the following suggestions for remodelers who are considering showrooms:

"First, determine if you have the volume to justify the showroom. The expenses can add up. In addition to the displays, you'll have increased rent, utilities, and insurance. Be sure you've covered it all.

"Next, decide if you'll be open all of the time accepting walk-in traffic or if your clients can use the showroom on an appointment-only basis. We are open limited hours, from 11 a.m. to 5 p.m., six days a week. One of our salespeople staffs the showroom each day. Any customers who walk in that day belong to that salesperson.

"Third, choose your vendors carefully. We recommend selecting well-established, large companies as your main suppliers. Sometimes you'll get a great deal from a company trying to break into the United States market, but, too often, they're around for a year and then gone, leaving you holding the bag.

"Choose one or two main suppliers in each area and try to mainly sell their products. You'll receive much better service and offers if you're a bigger player instead of being a small nobody to everyone.

"Last, when designing your showroom, stay away from trendy materials. They look great now, but will quickly become outdated. Then you'll be forced to spend more to redo your showroom.

If you use timeless designs and materials, you only have to update one or two displays each year to keep your showroom looking fresh and current. We spend between $10,000 and $30,000 to update our showroom each year. "

TRICKS OF THE TRADE FOR CREATING A GREAT SHOWROOM

- ▶ Identify your customers before you invest in a showroom. What market will you service—replacement kitchens and baths or custom remodeling? Build your showroom to fit your customers' profile, whether you only serve homeowners or work with architects and interior designers.

- ▶ Locate your showroom in a high-traffic area near other retail outlets. This will encourage walk-in traffic.

- ▶ Design your showroom to create product packages that will translate into easy sales. If you're selling replacement kitchens to condo owners, then build a vignette that will fit 90% of the condos in your market. Price it to be affordable to that market.

- ▶ Budget properly in the planning stages. Remember to account for overhead, the cost of the sales staff, and continual retrofitting. Determine just how many sales you must make to cover these costs. This will tell you if you can afford to build a showroom.

- ▶ Create packages for low-, medium-, and high-end budgets. Bundle together all of the elements a remodeled kitchen and bath needs and price the package attractively.

- ▶ Prepare clear, distinctive signage that's easily visible to people driving or walking by.

While a dynamite showroom can take you to a new level, take a realistic look at the large time and money investment it takes to make this tactic work. A showroom can be a wonderful sales and marketing tool, but it requires a commitment to do it right.

▲ *This is one of the beautiful vignettes featured in the Sea Pointe Construction showroom.*

YELLOW PAGES: HOW MUCH SHOULD YOU SPEND?

Advertising in the Yellow Pages is very successful for some companies and a total waste of money for others. Here are the benefits of this marketing tactic:

▸ Unlike people who browse through newspapers and magazines, many Yellow Pages shoppers have already decided to purchase a product or service.

- Yellow Pages are provided to everyone in a local area who has a phone.

- Yellow Pages are widely used and have the potential to generate a considerable number of leads for your company.

- Yellow Pages are also an important "phone book" for the shopper who knows about your company but doesn't have the phone number or address. Every company should have at least a minimal listing the Yellow Pages—it's usually free.

- A Yellow Pages ad includes a company's logo and "look," which may remind prospects that they do know about your company. When they see your ad, they may recall that you just did a job down the street in their neighborhood and that they've seen your truck signs a number of times.

And here are some cons:

- Yellow Pages shoppers have many companies and phone numbers at their fingertips, and just might be using those fingers to search out the lowest-priced company. They're often shopping around.

- Your ad is surrounded by your competitors' and may divert some of your prospects.

- The Yellow Pages is neither timely nor flexible; you're forced to make an advertising decision that will span an entire year.

- The positioning of your ad depends on seniority and size. The largest—and most expensive—ads go first in each category.

- The number of Yellow Pages books and categories are proliferating. You may have to invest in ads located in more than one category and more than one book to cover your market area.

There's no doubt that this is one of the most complex, difficult, and inflexible marketing decisions you will ever have to make. Before you invest any money in Yellow Pages advertising, ask yourself:

- Do you want just a simple listing?

- Do you want a display ad?

- Are you going to add color? (Studies show that responses increase with color, but not enough to offset the increased price.)

- How many categories will you appear in and in how many books will your ad be placed?

Researchers Doug Berdie and Elaine Hauff surveyed the buying habits of 946 consumers who were asked to choose businesses, including remodelers, from the Yellow Pages. Their report, "The Yellow Pages Report: A Comprehensive Guide for Advertisers," presents these findings:

Previous awareness of a company was the most important factor in choosing a contractor. The second most important factor was ad size. The third most important factor was ad content.

The business' location, which is vitally important for many types of companies, was not considered an important factor in choosing a contractor. However, if the consumer is looking for a showroom, location is likely to be a factor.

Consumers stressed the following factors as important in choosing a contractor's services:

- The length of time the company had been in business

- The brand names it sold

- Its licensing and bonding

- Whether or not the company offered financing
- Relevant professional associations
- The availability of free estimates.

Choose the most effective ad size for your company. Berdie and Hauff suggest that you:

- Review your local Yellow Pages for the last two to four years to assess your competitors' ad sizes.

- Choose an ad size to meet those competitors.

- Save money by purchasing $2/3$-page ads instead of full-page, or $3/8$-page ads instead of $1/2$-page ads. Increase the ad size from $1/4$ to $3/8$-page if your budget allows for it.

- Buy a larger ad instead of spending more on a color ad.

When a prospective customer says he or she found you in the Yellow Pages, be sure to ask whether the prospect knows about your company from any other source. Try to separate the true Yellow Pages lead from the lead who simply looked up your number there.

Consider adding a separate phone line and put that new number in the Yellow Pages. Then you'll automatically find out how those leads came to call you. And, lastly, be sure to track the number of Yellow Pages leads you receive and their conversion-to-sales rate.

HOSTING A RADIO TALK SHOW

More and more remodelers are becoming celebrities in their communities by hosting radio shows that focus on remodeling. Consumer interest in home improvement, decorating, and landscaping is skyrocketing, so nearly every talk-format radio station in the country has a show or two that addresses these topics.

If you're interested in hosting your own program, first do some research. Are there similar programs on radio stations in your market? What formats are they using—call-in, interviews on air? Could you try out radio by volunteering to be a guest?

Your best bet for a first-time show is a smaller station. Many of the smaller stations are looking for creative ideas for good shows. The shows must attract advertisers, who supply the station with revenue, as well as listeners.

Before you approach a radio station, prepare a proposal that describes the format you'll use and the audience you'll target. Show them that you're serious by including statistics on the size of the local remodeling market and growth patterns of the nationwide remodeling industry. These figures will demonstrate that remodeling is growing by leaps and bounds, and a show dedicated to the topic will be very popular.

Once you have a contract to do the show, convey your celebrity status throughout the rest of your marketing efforts. Send your customers regular invitations to listen to the program and include promotional material about it in all your presentation materials.

STREET SMARTS

Rosie Romero is the host of *Rosie on the House,* a call-in home improvement show broadcast from KTAR Radio in Scottsdale, Ariz., that reaches more than 80,000 homes throughout the area. Rosie has been hosting his show for about 15 years. "We were blessed with being in the right place at the right time," he says, "and I invested two years of family weekends into making this work. But it's paid off wonderfully."

Rosie was the owner of Legacy Custom Builders, Inc., a full-line remodeling company in Scottsdale, when he started his radio program. Here he offers some tips for making a success of it in today's radio show market.

Hosting a radio show is a great way to give your company instant credibility," Rosie says, "but it's not easy getting established. To be successful, you have to find the right station on which to launch your show. When I started it was a novel concept, but now every major station has at least one call-in home improvement show. You have to search out a station that doesn't and offer your services."

"Rosie initially did his show free for the radio station. He didn't get paid, and he didn't have to pay the station to air his show. "Now you almost have to buy your own airtime to get established," he says. "Once ratings start coming in, the story may change." Since Rosie's show is now the top weekend talk show in Arizona, "we can make the rules," he says. Hosts of successful home-improvement shows may never earn big bucks, but they may earn some compensation.

Straightforward information is not enough to hold listeners' interest in today's market. "You have to be entertaining; it's almost more important than the information. People want to be amused if they're going to invest time in your show," Rosie says.

Another caveat: "When we began our show, our main clients were upscale, affluent homeowners," he says. "But a call-in show drove us into the middle market. We had to be very careful not to alienate our existing customers while we built a market with new people."

Over the years, this radio show has generated thousands of leads for Rosie's company and for dozens of his preferred subcontractors. Rosie has become a celebrity in his home town!

■ ■ ■

USING CO-OP ADVERTISING

Remodelers often neglect the availability of co-op advertising funds for advertising. Building product manufacturers and/or distributors offer co-op funds to contractors who sell or use their products. The money is used to support and expand the contractors' marketing efforts.

Statistics show that less than 50% of co-op funds are used throughout the course of a year. The unused funds revert to the manufacturer or distributor each. Few remodelers know about these funds and know how to take advantage of them.

A co-op allocation often depends on the amount of materials you've purchased in a year—usually from one manufacturer (for instance windows, or siding). Most companies don't set limits on funds but require any ad, brochure, or postcard to be approved by their marketing department before they will provide funds. Co-op funds often can be used for in-house marketing pieces as well as newspaper, magazine, and radio advertising.

To receive co-op funds, you may be asked to meet stringent requirements. However, the manufacturer's logo you must place on your ad is often small and unobtrusive. Using this method, you can produce a marketing piece for your company at half the normal cost.

Even if a manufacturer doesn't offer cash to defray the cost, they'll often offer ready-to-use marketing materials such as brochures, postcards, ad slicks, radio commercials, and entire direct mail programs. These professionally created marketing materials have been tested and created specifically for remodelers.

Ask your manufacturer or distributor representative for information on the marketing materials and co-op advertising funds they have available.

Sue Ladd, operations manager of Excel Interior Concepts & Construction in Lemoyne, Pa., finds and collects over $25,000 in co-op advertising funds each year. She says, "It was a headache to get started, but now it's paying off very well."

Sue suggests remodelers start with their local lumberyard or other building product distributor to locate available advertising programs and funds. "It's not easy to find the information," says Sue. "You have to dig and be persistent. Right now, we receive co-op from our cabinet company, a major plumbing manufacturer, and a window manufacturer. I'm now digging to find other funds from another product category—like flooring."

Co-op money doesn't always come quickly. Sue says, "Once you learn the manufacturer's system—who approves the ad, what materials to send for approval, how to submit the proof of the ad, and who to go to if payment doesn't come—things become much easier. Some manufacturers pay quickly, and some I have to bug."

Excel Interior Concepts & Construction recently received $26,000 from one window manufacturer. The money paid for half of the cost of a large, colorful billboard located on a busy, nearby highway. "We stumbled upon this money," says Sue. "In a conversation with a representative from our lumberyard, we discovered that no one had used the co-op dollars provided by the manufacturer, so we jumped on it. They helped us create and pay for the billboard—something we definitely would not have done without this infusion of cash."

■ ■ ■

UNIVERSE MARKETING PLAN AND BUDGET

The universe portion of your marketing program reaches out beyond your past customers and those prospects who have the same demographics as your current buyers. You want universe marketing efforts to reach the next circle of potential buyers. Note: If you're a small company, your lead generation needs will probably be satisfied with the first two parts of your program—and you won't need to spend anything on the universe segment.

TACTICS/EFFORTS COST

Newspaper	$ _____
Magazine	$ _____
Radio	$ _____
Television	$ _____
Home/mall shows	$ _____
Award program entries	$ _____
Publicity	$ _____
Networking	$ _____
Showroom	$ _____
Yellow Pages	$ _____
Consumer seminars	$ _____
Adult education course	$ _____
Charitable events	$ _____
Remodeled homes tour	$ _____
Radio talk show	$ _____
Other _____	$ _____
_____	$ _____
TOTAL BUDGET	$ _____

part six

PUTTING IT ALL TOGETHER

Marketing Tactics and Budget

Marketing Calendar

Putting it all Together

Sample Marketing Calendar

Your Marketing Calendar

The big moment has arrived. Now, it's time to pick and choose from the marketing menu that we've presented. Before you begin, take a look at last year's lead generation performance to find out what worked for you. Which efforts delivered the high-quality leads you were looking for? Highlight the winners and drop the losers.

Now choose the variety of tactics that will provide the best avenues to reach your targeted audience for the most affordable investment. Remember, you have to spend money to make money. Don't hold back on a tactic that could deliver big results. At the same time, don't put all your hopes (and money) on one tactic. Think diversity.

Go back to Part 1 to review your company goals and the number of leads you need to attract during the year.

MARKETING TACTICS AND BUDGET

From the exercises you've already completed, you know your marketing program will hit your three main audiences: Circle of Influence, prospects, and universe. Once you've chosen the tactics you'll use to reach these groups, it's time to put them all together. Here's a sample marketing program you can use as a guide. It's not a one-size-fits-all formula. You must create the special mix of tactics that will work for your company. Use approximate budget numbers at this stage. You can fine-tune them later.

SAMPLE MARKETING PROGRAM

Projected sales volume: $1,500,000

Marketing budget (2% of annual volume): $30,000

Average job size: $50,000

You will need to produce 30 jobs a year to reach your goals.

If you close 1 out of 8 raw leads, you will need 240 raw leads a year. This means you will need to attract 20 raw leads a month.

Qualified leads are those prospects that you feel could be a good fit with your company. Typically, you feel it's worth your time to make an appointment with the prospect.

If you close 1 out of 4 qualified leads, you will need 120 qualified leads for the year. This means you will need 10 qualified leads a month.

COMPANY MATERIALS BUDGET

Update logo	$2,000.00
Develop brochure	1,800.00
Paint one truck	1,800.00
Business cards for lead carpenters	100.00
Uniforms	300.00
Upgrade web site	2,500.00
SUB-TOTAL	**$ 8,500.00**

CIRCLE OF INFLUENCE PROGRAM

Thank-you notes	$ 50.00
Customer gifts	1,200.00
Four mailings	500.00
SUB-TOTAL	**$1,750.00**

PROSPECT PROGRAM

Job site mailings	$2,500.00
Freelance assistance	1,000.00
Upgrade job sign (including labor to build sign)	250.00
One showroom seminar	4,730.00
SUB-TOTAL	**$8,480.00**

UNIVERSE PROGRAM

Float in 4th of July parade	$1,500.00
Networking through professional memberships (dues, regular meetings	660.00
Yellow Pages listing	2,000.00
Ad in softball league directory	250.00
SUB-TOTAL	**$4,410.00**
Contingency fund*	$3,000.00

Many companies set aside a 5 to 10% contingency fund so they can take advantage of special opportunities that may crop up during the year (e.g., special event sponsorship, media advertising special sections, or customer appreciation events).

Staff to implement plan	$3,860.00
TOTAL	**$30,000.00**

CREATING AN ACTION PLAN

You need to create an action plan to produce and implement the marketing tactics you've planned. Consider:

▸ How will the program be done?

▸ How will it be improved from last year?

▸ Who will be in charge?

▸ What it will cost?

▸ When will it be completed?

▸ What will be used?

▸ What needs to be produced and when will it be utilized?

▸ How will you measure the program's effectiveness or success?

YOUR MARKETING BUDGET

Using the exercises in the previous sections in this book, complete the following:

Marketing budget total for the year	$_____
Materials development budget	$_____
Circle of Influence budget	$_____
Prospect marketing budget	$_____
Universe marketing budget	$_____
Other	$_____
Other	$_____
Other	$_____
Contingency budget (10%)	$_____
Staff to Implement	$_____
TOTAL	**$_____**

Are you within budget? If not, identify those tactics that are most important to the successful lead generation for the company and cut the rest. Under budget? Great! Add another great tactic or two!

MARKETING CALENDAR

By the beginning of each fiscal year, create a marketing calendar that includes all the tactics in your marketing plan. Although a marketing calendar is an adaptable document that's subject to change throughout the year, it will give you a strong "roadmap" of tactics to follow. This map can then be handed off to someone else to do much of the actual implementation.

A marketing calendar shows you how you can spread your marketing expenditures throughout the year to avoid a major drain on your cash flow. It also encourages you prepare yourself for certain tasks that need to be done each month. A caveat: When cash flow is low because of slow sales, you may need to spend additional marketing dollars to generate new business.

Transfer the variety of tactics you have planned for the year onto a master marketing calendar, which will be your overall roadmap for the year's lead generation program. Review this calendar frequently to make sure you're staying on top of the various marketing tactics. Go back to the particular project sheet for the details of each tactic.

Ongoing Marketing Efforts

Database upkeep
Send customer evaluations
Job site marketing
Collect testimonials
Customer gifts for referrals
Use "Why we lost the job" surveys
Attend town meetings

Here's a sample marketing calendar. It's nothing fancy, but gives you a feel for the flow of tactics throughout the course of the year.

SAMPLE MARKETING CALENDAR

JANUARY

Build home show booth

Build doll house for giveaway

Design/write/print newsletter #1

FEBRUARY

Mail Circle of Influence newsletter #1

Mail press release #1

Home & Garden Show

MARCH

Plan open house

Have invitations designed

APRIL

Send open house invitations

Order open house refreshments

Send special invitation to media

MAY

Design/write/print newsletter #2

Open house May 17

Mail press release #2

JUNE

Schedule photographer

Co-op ad research

Circle of Influence newsletter #2

JULY

Begin direct mail project research

Get rules for award entry

AUGUST

Circle of Influence mailing #3

Home show at fair

SEPTEMBER

Have pro photos taken—
award, press releases

Develop award entry

Direct mail to Hillsdale area

Design Thanksgiving cards

OCTOBER

Send in award entry

Purchase sweatshirts for crew

Print Thanksgiving cards

NOVEMBER

Thanksgiving mailing—

Circle of Influence #4

Press release #3

Select/purchase client gifts

DECEMBER

Send/deliver client holiday gifts

✏️ YOUR MARKETING CALENDAR

Now it's time to schedule your own marketing tactics month-by-month. Use the form below or use your own calendar to document the tactics that should occur in each month.

JANUARY

_____

_____

_____

FEBRUARY

_____

_____

_____

MARCH

_____

_____

_____

APRIL

_____

_____

_____

MAY

_____

_____

_____

JUNE

_____

_____

_____

JULY

_____

_____

_____

AUGUST

_____

_____

_____

SEPTEMBER

_____

_____

_____

OCTOBER

_____

_____

_____

NOVEMBER

_____

_____

_____

DECEMBER

_____

_____

_____

ONGOING MARKETING EFFORTS

_____

_____

_____

_____

part seven

TRACK YOUR MARKETING SUCCESS

Monitoring Your Leads and Sales

Lost Jobs: Finding Out Why

What Do Your Customers Really Think?

Customer Evaluation Cover Letter

Customer Evaluation Questionnaire

MONITORING YOUR LEADS AND SALES

Information is the key to continual improvement—and continual improvement is the key to staying ahead of the competition. But information doesn't just happen. It takes a concerted effort to gather this knowledge from all of the sources that can contribute to your company's overall success. These sources include lead generation statistics, sales statistics, job size averages, customer information, and feedback from prospects who didn't purchase from your company.

The smartest, savviest remodelers don't leave anything to chance. They work to uncover as much as they can about the trends in their company. If you're not tracking your leads, asking your customers how they felt about your work, or finding out why you weren't hired, you're missing out on an essential element of your business. Let's talk about some systems that can help you track these important data. There's an old saying, "That which is measured, gets done. You must measure that which is important to your success."

Measuring your marketing results ensures that the right program gets implemented. It also lets you know whether your marketing investment is being well spent.

TRACK YOUR MARKETING SUCCESS

To start off on the right foot, gather data on where your leads are coming from—what is their source? Each time a new prospect calls, ask for essential marketing information using a hard-copy sales lead form or a software program that manages contacts. Gathering this information will help you in two ways:

Tracking your marketing results. To determine if your marketing is working, keep track of where the leads are coming from, which tactic attracted them, and the types of projects that the prospects want to create. For example, the local home show may have only produced 50 leads but they're all high-quality, desirable prospects. That's great.

In comparison, the Yellow Pages may generate 300 leads, but these prospects may be price shoppers, or asking for work that's outside your niche. These are undesirable leads. By having this information available, you'll see that you should drop the display ad in the Yellow Pages and invest in another home show. Without tracking every single lead that finds its way to your office, you'll never know what's really working and what's not.

Pre-qualifying leads. For all entrepreneurs—and especially remodelers—time is money. At one time or another, we've all found ourselves meeting with people who turn out to be poor prospects. In fact, sometimes we sense that people are poor prospects during the first telephone call. Every time you use your limited sales time to meet with unqualified prospects, you're taking time away from other, more productive tasks. It's up to you to make sure that you have a reasonable chance of closing a job before you go on an appointment. If there's little chance of selling a job, spend your time improving your marketing or selling to better leads. If your lead generation program is attracting too many unqualified leads, it needs to be reworked.

SAMPLE LEAD FORM

Use a rating system to quickly sort good prospects from mediocre ones. The sample lead form below gives each lead a numeric value by letting you add up the rankings in two categories: lead source and type of project. The value you assign to different types of projects depends on your company's niche, so customize this form and the numeric rating system to fit your company.

Date _____   Salesperson _____

Name _____

Address _____

City_____State _____ Zip _____

Home Phone _____

Office Phone_____

Lead Source

How did you hear about our company? (Circle one number)

45 Repeat customer

45 Referral from previous customer (Who?)

45 Referral from friend of company (Who?)

35 Read about company in newspaper or other publication

35 Received job site marketing piece or saw job site sign

30 Attended open house

25 Received direct mail piece

20 Saw company advertisement (Where?)

10 Visited booth at trade show (Which show?)

0 Chose company from Yellow Pages

0 Other

Type of Project

What type of project are you considering? (Circle one)

45 New home

35 Major remodeling,

45 Addition including kitchen

30 Kitchen remodel

20 Bath remodel

15 Basement remodeling

How long have you lived in your home?

Have you remodeled before? ☐ Yes ☐. No If yes, how was the experience? _____

Who was your contractor?

What research have you done on this project?

Do you have an investment range in mind? ($ to $)

Add up the points from the two categories on this form. The total score indicates the lead's quality. Here's a key for interpreting scores:
65-90 Excellent   45-64 Good   20-44 Fair   Below 20 Poor

If you are using a hard-copy form, reproduce it on colored paper so it's easy to identify and less likely to get lost. Some remodelers use three-part lead forms: One copy goes into a master lead book, one goes to the sales manager, and the third goes to the salesperson.

Some software programs let you enter, save, and track all this information on your computer. Using the initial data, you can customize form letters and mail them at various intervals. The data is then moved over into the job file when the project is sold. When the project is complete, the client's name and other pertinent data moves into your Circle of Influence list.

TRACKING LEADS AND SALES

Monitoring the results of your lead generation program lets you use your money and time to attract highly targeted leads for just the kind of profitable work you want.

Effective monitoring is more than counting the number of leads you receive. You must review the cost associated with each tactic and—most importantly—analyze the lead-to-sale conversion rate. Checking the average sales price of all the sales created by a certain lead generation tactic yields another telling statistic. For instance, Yellow Pages leads might generate sales that average $11,080, while your home show leads might average sales of $15,837. That's an important difference in quality that will affect how you allocate your marketing money next year.

When you can measure the effectiveness of any marketing tactic using the four criteria below, you are taking charge of your marketing. You will make informed decisions on which lead generation tactics work and which don't.

▸ Quantity of leads generated

▸ Per-lead cost

▸ Conversion rate (closing rate) of leads into sales

▸ Average size of sale

Use this simple form to track your lead and sales information quarterly and annually. Many remodelers use lead/sales-tracking software. Just be sure you gather and keep this information because it's key to maintaining a successful marketing program.

Whether they're good, bad, hot, or ugly, leads are loaded with vital information that can tell contractors a lot about their remodeling firms. Jeffrey A. Titus, general manager for Titus Built, LLC in Wilton, Conn., uses a spreadsheet to track where his leads come from, when they came in, if a proposal was given, and if it resulted in a job.

"It helps us so we don't have some people fall through the cracks. It also tells us where we should be focusing our efforts," Titus says. "If we know how many leads we need to sell a job and how many proposals we need to get a sale, we'll know how many leads we need to generate."

The system enables Titus to identify which past clients are giving referrals. In addition, tracking the leads from year to year allows the company to chart its progress and set benchmarks and goals.

"If we know how much time it takes from the initial contact to a proposal to a job, it'll help with our sales projections. When we look at that information at the end of the year, we'll see if we need to change the hit ratio of the number of leads to the number of jobs," Titus says. "Tracking the leads doesn't take a lot of time, and knowing where your leads are coming from is a lot better than not knowing."

■ ■ ■

LEAD AND SALES TRACKING FORM

Source	# of Leads	$ Expense per Lead	# of Appts.	$/Appt	# of Sales	$/Sale	Avg. Job	Closing Conversion Rate
Repeat business								
Referrals								
Job site signs								
Vehicle signs								
Canvassing								
Direct mail to jobsites								
Yellow Pages								
Publicity								
Newspaper ads								
Magazine ads								
Radio								
Television								
Home shows								
Mall shows								
Telemarketing								
Direct mail								
Web site								
Other:								
TOTAL								

Sample entry:

Source	# of Leads	$ Expense per lead	# of Appts.	$/Appt	# of Sales	$/Sale	Avg. Job	Closing Conversion Rate
Newspaper Ads **$1800**	45	$40	18	$100	6	$300	$65,400	13%

This sample entry shows that our company placed small newspaper ads throughout the year for a total expenditure of $1,800. Here are the results of that expenditure:

- These ads generated 45 leads.

- Dividing $1,800 by 45 showed us our average lead cost was $40.00

- From those leads, we made 18 appointments.

- Dividing $1,800 by 18 tells us that we spent $100 per appointment

- From those leads, we sold 6 jobs, or 1 out of three leads.

- $1,800 divided by 6 tells us we invested $300 for each sale.

- Because we closed six of the 45 leads, our closing conversion rate is 13%

- The 6 sales averaged $65,400 each.

LOST JOBS: FINDING OUT WHY

You'll often hear about the wonderful reasons why a customer chose your company, but you'll rarely find out why someone didn't choose you. That information can be even more important. Surveying a would-be client to find out why you lost a job can pay off by helping you improve your company's services—and that can mean more leads.

This survey should be short (no more than two sides) and should be quick and easy to complete. Include a stamped, self-addressed envelope to encourage a response. Consider offering a small gift or a contribution to charity if the respondent sends back the completed survey. You should send the survey form to all prospects who did not award your company their business.

Here is a sample survey with explanations (in italics) of why certain questions are important:

"Why We Didn't Get the Job" SURVEY

Thank you for the opportunity to consult with you on your remodeling project. It is important to us that we deliver the best service and highest quality product available. If you would take a moment to tell us why you did not choose our company, it would greatly help our efforts to improve. We appreciate your help.

1. Have you awarded your remodeling contract to another remodeling company? ☐ Yes
   If yes, could you give us the name of the remodeling company who was awarded the job? (Optional)

Information on competitors will help you keep an eye on the marketplace and your competitive situation. Are there new companies coming into your area that might affect your business? Are existing companies expanding their range of services?

☐ No (Please move to question 4).

Prospects often put remodeling projects on hold for various reasons. Unfortunately, many remodelers lose touch with these prospects and lose their opportunity to sell them when the prospect decides to go forward with the project. Determining whether or not the job has been awarded is a first step in deciding whether or not to stay in touch with prospects who may be on the fence. This allows you to keep undecided prospects in your database and continue to market to them.

2. Was your decision based on any of the following? If more than one, please number in order of importance.

_____ Timeliness of response

_____ Salesperson's ability to accurately assess your needs

_____ Company's ability to present creative solutions

_____ Clarity and completeness of our proposal to you

_____ Professionalism of our presentation

_____ Personal rapport with salesperson

_____ Previous relationship with company

_____ Product offerings

_____ Company's reputation

_____ Price.

This question will help you uncover factors that gave another company the competitive edge. If you're competing against the same companies again and again, this information will help you identify the specific areas in which you need to improve.

3. If price was a factor, was our company's proposal higher than another company's proposals by:

☐ 0-5%

☐ 6-9%

☐ 10-15%

☐ More than 15%

☐ Other

_____

_____

_____

Remodelers often try justify a prospect's rejection by assuming the decision was based on price. Don't assume. Find out if price was indeed an issue and, if so, how much of an issue. Because the remodeling industry is extremely competitive, you should be sensitive to the pricing issue and be aware of what your competitors are charging.

4. How many times did you meet with the other company's representative?

_____

Did the other remodeler give away huge chunks of valuable time in his/her attempt to capture the business? Did the salesperson close on the second meeting or were there five or six meetings before the prospect made a decision?

5. If you did not proceed at all, why not?

_____

_____

May we contact you in the future? ☐ Yes   ☐ No

6. Please rate our company representative on the following:
Ability to listen and understand your needs
Poor I   2   3   4   5   Excellent

Professional appearance
Poor I   2   3   4   5   Excellent

Remodelers differ in their opinions concerning the best clothing to wear to a sales call. Make sure that prospects perceive you and your salespeople as the professionals you are. If you receive low professional appearance scores, upgrade your appearance for a few months and monitor the changes in these results.

Presentation of company and proposal

Poor 1 2 3 4 5 Excellent

Technical expertise

Poor 1 2 3 4 5 Excellent

Was the client satisfied that you knew what you were talking about? Were you able to answer the questions that came up? It's important that your salespeople be experienced enough to thoroughly and confidently answer common questions. If this area receives a poor mark often, you may consider taking action to bring his or her knowledge up to your standards.

Quality of our solutions

Poor 1 2 3 4 5 Excellent

Timeliness of response

Poor 1 2 3 4 5 Excellent

Additional comments

_____

_____

_____

_____

Leave room for unsolicited comments. Often, the most telling information will be provided here. Every salesperson has their good points and their bad points. Find out what your salesperson does right and the areas he or she is weak in. Then work to improve the weak areas. This information also gives you the opportunity to compare salespeople within your organization and to monitor a particular salesperson's improvements.

WHAT DO YOUR CUSTOMERS REALLY THINK?

Keep tabs on the quality of your services by asking your clients to complete a questionnaire after their jobs are finished. This will help you improve those areas in which you're weak. Continually monitoring your customers also lets you measure your steps toward improvement.

Make the customer evaluation questionnaire easy to complete. Enclose the form with a cover letter and a stamped, self-addressed envelope. Don't expect 100% response—30% to 40% is typical. You may be able to improve response by offering a free gift or a small contribution to charity for clients who send their evaluations to you. If you don't receive a response, mail a second evaluation. Follow up with a telephone call if the response is not returned.

Once you receive a completed evaluation, send a thank-you note or call the clients to thank them for taking the time to help you. On a quarterly basis, determine the average scores for each of the questions and the total for the 10 numeric questions. Then compare the scores to the previous quarter to see if your company is improving. These averages will also give you a reading of your employees' effectiveness. For example, if the score for question 2 is consistently low, you'll know that's a major problem. If you see a sudden drop in a score, correct the problem before it becomes serious.

CUSTOMER EVALUATION COVER LETTER

Dear (customer's name),

Thanks again for your business. We appreciate your confidence in us. To continue to earn business from wonderful people like you, we are always working to improve our services and procedures. Would you please help us in our efforts by giving us your feedback on your recently completed project?

Enclosed is a short survey that rates us in a variety of areas. Of course, we'd also like any other comments—positive or negative. Constructive criticism is very beneficial.

Thanks for helping us become the best remodeling company we can be!

Cordially,
(Your name)

P.S. If there's anything we can do for you, please don't hesitate to call.

CUSTOMER EVALUATION QUESTIONNAIRE

Name (Optional)

As you circle your ratings, please remember that a "5" rating is excellent; a "1" rating is poor.

1. How happy are you with the project design?	1	2	3	4	5
2. Was our salesperson courteous and helpful?	1	2	3	4	5
3. Was the design process smooth?	1	2	3	4	5
4. Was our salesperson knowledgeable?	1	2	3	4	5
5. Was our office staff friendly and efficient?	1	2	3	4	5

6. Were we accessible when you phoned,   1   2   3   4   5
   and timely about returning your calls?

7. Was our production manager responsive to your   1   2   3   4   5
   concerns and questions?

8. How would you rate the people working   1   2   3   4   5
   on your job?

9. Were our subcontractors professional and   1   2   3   4   5
   quality-conscious?

10. Did we clean up as expected?   1   2   3   4   5

11. How was our overall performance?   1   2   3   4   5

12. What did you like best about working with us?

13. In what areas should we concentrate our efforts to improve?

14. Additional comments. (If you rated us poorly on any section, we'd appreciate any specific comments relating to our performance in that area.)

_____

_____

15. Do you know a friend, neighbor, or business associate who could benefit from our services? (Optional)

The following information is optional as well:

Name

Address

City, State/Zip

Thank You!

resources

TWELVE READY-TO-GO CONSUMER NEWSLETTER ARTICLES

Here are 12 sample articles that are perfect for plugging into a newsletter aimed at your Circle of Influence. Use them as they are or edit them to fit your company's needs. If you don't have time for a newsletter, simply print one of these articles on your letterhead and send it along with a note saying "I thought you might find this interesting."

Basements with Flair

Looking for space to put an exercise room, entertainment center, or playroom? Go underground! If your home has an unfinished basement, remodeling might be a great way to transform this commonly under-used space.

When considering a basement remodel, start by making a floor plan. Be sure to mark the location of your furnace, washer and dryer, and any other large appliances. Take notes on:
- Access to the basement from upstairs and outside
- Location of existing plumbing if you want an additional bathroom
- Location of vertical support columns
- Location of windows and doors
- Floor/ceiling/wall materials

Given their constant contact with the earth, basements are vulnerable to dampness, which makes basement remodeling a bit more complex than first meets the eye. We'll help you take appropriate measures to ensure a room free from moisture.

Most basements have low ceilings and few windows. But this doesn't have to limit you. There are many creative ways to make your basement light and airy. Talk to us about the variety of wall and ceiling lighting options available. We'll make sure to provide appropriate electrical lines and outlets.

Here are some tricks-of-the-trade for making your underground space first-class:

- Stay away from dark wood paneling and instead consider drywall painted in light tones to make the room brighter. Semi-gloss paint will gently reflect even more light into the room.

- Open up the visual space. Double doors—even glass double interior doors—take away the typical cubicle look. Or, how about a rounded archway or pass-through area from one room into another?

- Check to see if existing windows can be enlarged. Or, consider installing a small boxed window for a mini-garden to grow herbs or start plant seedlings.

- Built-in bookcases and entertainment units add richness and depth to a room. Light them with interior lights or from the top to cast light downwards.

- Disguise vertical support beams and horizontal ceiling pipes or floor joists by boxing them in. Or, you might decide to actually use pipes and beams as interesting accents by painting them with bold colors or subtle earth tones.

An unfinished basement is much like a diamond in the rough—unexplored splendor awaiting your discovery!

2 Giving Your Bathroom a Facelift

Nothing dates a house more quickly than a bathroom that time has forgotten. Yet drab or outdated bathrooms can be dramatically revitalized. Bath products abound that can give you as lavish a bathroom as you could possibly want. Many homeowners want their bathrooms to be totally utilitarian, but others want rooms in which to pamper themselves. How about you?

Your answer, and your budget, will determine the best way to remodel. Do you want to work within the existing space of your current bathroom? Do you want to expand by taking room from somewhere else? Would you rather build an addition to accommodate your new bath? These are are just a few options which vary greatly in cost.

Renovating your current space is usually the least complicated and least expensive option. While the layout of your existing bathroom can be altered to some extent, moving major plumbing fixtures is the most costly aspect of a remodel. Local building codes require minimum clearances between, beside, and in front of fixtures to allow for use, cleaning, and repair.

If you have an extra bedroom, you could move the bathroom to this space or expand a current bath into a portion of it. This will mean moving the plumbing but it will also add a modern, spacious bathroom to your home which will increase the resale value. An addition or even a small bump-out could be the solution. This requires the largest investment but will give you just what you want.

If you've decided to remodel, start with an analysis of your existing bathroom:

- What is the condition of the sink, toilet, and tub/shower? If it's an older, wall-hanging toilet, you might update the look, perhaps with a low-water consumption style. If your tub is basically sound, consider reglazing it. However, many home-owners are moving up to whirlpool style tubs.

• Does the sink have a vanity for storage? If it does, but you just don't like it, consider replacing it with a one of the many beautiful varieties that are available today.

• Does the sink have independent faucets? If so, you know how inconvenient this can be. Why not switch to a single oper-ating lever which is easier to use and gives a better mix of temperatures?

• Does your tub include a shower? One can easily be added with a combination tub-shower valve.

• Think about reinforcing the walls, adding grab bars, and widening doors for visitors with physical disabilities or for your later years.

• Is your medicine cabinet small and outdated? Consider the various styles of newer cabinets, perhaps with recessed or dec-orative lighting.

• How is the tile? If it is chipped and cracked and matching tile is not available, replacement or reglazing may be your best option.

• If a wooden window is suffering the effects of humidity, it may be best to replace it and older metal windows with new vinyl windows. Deco glass block has made a comeback and is a good option for adding light and design flair to a bathroom.

• Many older bathrooms don't have adequate ventilation. You may want to add a fan to avoid moisture build-up which can deteriorate materials and promote the growth of mold and mildew.

• Are electrical outlets a problem? Face it, the number of electrical appliances we use in our daily rituals has multiplied since the time many houses were built. That means that you probably want more outlets. New and replacement ones should be protected ground fault circuit interrupter (GFCI) outlets that are made to shut off automatically when they sense water.

Today's bathroom can be all you want it to be. Enjoy the opportunity to explore the variety of materials, styles, and colors available to you. In the end, you'll have a well-designed bathroom that functions as beautifully as it looks.

3 Unfinished Attics are Remodeling Opportunities

Need more living space or storage room? If the answer is yes, look up! If you have an unfinished attic, your problem may be well on the way to being solved. Attic space already has a floor, walls, and roof, so it is an opportunity waiting to be used.

To be a good candidate for remodeling, attic space needs three important ingredients:
- Appropriate headroom
- Easy access
- Adequate floor joist support.

Headroom is of primary importance. Building codes require at least 7 1/2 feet of headroom between the peak of the roof and the floor. If you don't have this space, you can also raise the roof (which is a project for an entirely different column—and budget.)

Another important factor is how the attic space can be accessed. Will you have to carve the space for a stairway from an existing room? Or might your best choice be a pull-down staircase? (Building codes don't allow the use of a pull-down stair for main access) Think about the traffic patterns that will develop to and from the converted attic space.

One of the most important aspects of using your attic is the strength of the floor joists. Most ceilings are not designed with joists that can withstand the weight that a floor must handle. This means that the ceiling joists must be reinforced, which could be a complex process.

Before you begin, let's talk about the options. While you might be able to tackle some remodeling projects yourself, attic remodeling requires greater expertise. An attic conversion can provide your home with a uniquely designed space to serve a range of functions—an extra bedroom/bath suite, guest room, office, family room, exercise room, or hobby room. Look up and you'll never look back!

4 Make an Addition to Your Family

Homeowners never fail to be impressed by the difference major space changes can make in the quality of a family's life. You love your home, but it isn't working well for you. You don't want to leave your neighborhood, neighbors, and schools, but something must be done to refit your house to your lifestyle.

Not to worry. Adding a room, wing, or floor to your existing home might be a major undertaking, but it can also be a fulfilling experience—especially if the addition is well designed. Excellent design is critical since the project can either enhance or detract from your existing structure. The one thing you don't want is an addition that clashes with your home or sticks out like a sore thumb.

Begin by evaluating the style of your home. Is it contemporary or traditional? Is it a Victorian bungalow, rambler, split-level, or colonial? Each home style has specific architectural lines and details that can be echoed in your addition's design.

Take a look at your home's style. Pay special attention to the:
- Pitch of the roof;
- Style of windows and doors;
- Architectural details such as shutters, moldings, and porches;
- Materials used—type of shingles, siding, stone, brick, stucco.

Think about which architectural details you want to repeat in your addition's design. Repeating design elements is an excellent method of creating additions that look as though they had always been there. For example, your addition could include a dormer that mirrors another elsewhere on your home. And it should include a complementary window style to that of the original.

Next, think in terms of scale. A common design mistake is an addition that overshadows the original home or is much too small and insignificant to add to the overall architectural style. Cut out pictures of homes that you appreciate. This "homework" will help you zero in on your particular tastes.

The design of the interior offers more flexibility since it's not viewed in its entirety as the exterior is. Even so, you'll still want to strive for a comfortable transition from existing space to new. Ceiling style and height can make a big difference in the tone of a room. A steeply pitched roof on the exterior can make way for a dramatic cathedral ceiling on the interior. This can add drama to a contemporary or traditionally designed space in a living room, kitchen, bathroom, or family room.

Little is more satisfying than living in a house that's been beautifully remodeled with a new addition. If you've taken the time to plan carefully and pay attention to the details that make it part of your home, you'll love your new space more with each passing day.

5 Brighten Up With Bump-Outs!

Remodelers have long known that a small addition (a "bump-out") that enlarges an existing room can be a value-conscious remodeling project. Often that bump-out brightens your home more than a large addition.

Look around your home for cramped, dark areas that could be improved with a minimum-sized addition. Have you considered adding a walk-in bay window to your dining room? You'll be amazed at how this small change will open up and brighten the room. How about a deep window seat in your favorite room for a cozy reading nook? This can be designed to include hidden storage. Angled entrances can give you access to a little-used section of yard while allowing light to stream in. Have you been dreaming of a whirlpool in the bathroom? A bump-out would give you room for the new bath and an expanse of windows to add spaciousness.

Bump-outs may have a funny name, but they can add space, light, and interest to many rooms in your house. Call us today to discuss creative bump-out ideas for your home!

6 Kitchen and Bath Safety Audit

If you're a parent, you've already thought about minimizing or eliminating safety hazards in your bathroom and kitchen. With new, recently developed products, you can easily remove much of the risk. Start by taking a fresh look at your home while conducting a safety audit. Does your bathroom and kitchen have the following safety features?

Bathroom
- Slip-resistant strips in the tub and nearby to minimize the risk of slipping and falling
- Grab bars in tubs and showers
- Towels bars/rings close to the tub or shower
- Impact-resistant safety-glass or plastic tub/shower enclosure
- Shatter-resistant tub faucets that don't have sharp edges
- Recessed soap dishes (those that stick out from the wall can cause injury if a person falls against them)
- The new soft bathtub, which is made of impact-absorbing materials to reduce the risk of injury for young and old alike
- Non-slip tile to reduce the risk of falling on a wet surface
- Toilet latches to prevent children from opening the lid
- Electrical outlets designed to automatically cut off power in the presence of water contact or faulty circuitry
- Door hardware that can be unlocked from either side
- Temperature-controlled faucets to avoid serious skin burns (typical faucets can produce water that is more than 120 degrees F, which can scald a child's tender skin).

Kitchen
- A stove with top controls that are difficult for children to reach
- Appliances, sharp knives and other sharp objects kept out of sight and reach in appliance garages, in-drawer knifeblocks, and built-in storage units
- Slip/impact-resistant flooring
- Cabinet latches to keep children from dangerous products.

7 Remodeling Through Color

Did you know that the colors you select for your home have meaning and can set mood? Studies show that color can complement architecture, enhance or diminish the sense of space, create a particular ambience, and impact your daily moods. Color experts have studied how color is likely to affect you. Here is what they have found:

- Blue, universally a favorite, is recognized for its tranquil effects. However, if too dark or used too expansively, it can have a depressing effect.

- Red evokes excitement, and is an excellent accent. Often used in kitchens, it's felt that red enhances one's appetite.

- Green is either loved or heartily disliked, so take care when making this selection.

- Brown and orange are viewed as friendly and informal colors.

- Yellow, generally perceived as a cheery color, may make children feel depressed, so use it sparingly.

- Neutral colors can serve as dramatic backdrops for furnishings, collections, and accessories. Neutrals also add the flexibility to introduce new colors seasonally with throw pillows, artwork, and other decorative items.

When selecting your colors:

- Select exterior shades that harmonize with the home's surroundings—steer towards the earthier shades (e.g., a grey-blue vs. a bright royal blue).

- Consider the style and era of your home—there might be some traditional colors associated with them—especially with Victorian and traditional Colonials.

- When viewing paint samples, look at chip sizes proportionate to how they will ultimately be used (e.g., if a wall will be painted taupe with a red accent, view a larger sample of the taupe paint against a smaller sample of the red).

- Less is more. Don't overuse a color, especially in a small room.

- Even though a color may be too strong for an entire wall, consider it for an accent color.

- Most importantly, select colors that work for you and your lifestyle, not what's considered "in" or "out" at the time. But don't be afraid to color your world—you'll find it will make a world of difference!

8 How to Work With Your Contractor

Are you planning to remodel your home? If the answer is yes, here are some tips on how to establish and maintain a good working relationshop with your remodeling contractor.

Of course you believe you're a reasonable, understanding person with whom anyone would be happy to work. However, if you've never been involved with remodeling your home, you'd be surprised at what might happen!

Realistic Expectations

Everyone who begins the remodeling process has visions of the "dream" home they'll have when it's completed. Few, however, give much thought to the dust and dirt, noise, inconveniences, scheduling delays, and slight problems that must be dealt with along the way. These elements are part and parcel of any remodeling job, and every client must be realistic and accept the fact that there will be some inconveniences.

How inconvenient and unpleasant the process is depends a lot on the working relationship we create right from the beginning. A good client-contractor relationship depends on several things:

1. Be honest with us from the beginning about your expectations. Clear communication is the foundation of a successful project.

2. Be realistic about what you are looking for in the remodel and what you are willing to budget for the project. Many homeowners enter a remodeling project with grandiose plans that need to be scaled down to meet their budget. We'll work with you to provide you with the best your money can afford. But remember, this is our livelihood. As with any profession, some profit margin must be factored into the price.

3. Let's discuss our work schedule. If the schedule falls behind, feel free to ask why.

4. Realize that certain stages of remodeling may seem to go more quickly than others. For example, during stages that involve more tangible work (for example, when walls are being torn down or replaced, framing constructed, or appliances installed), you'll have a true sense of rapid progress. During other stages, however, that involve work of a more "hidden" nature like the installation of electrical lines or plumbing, it may seem that the work is going nowhere. Don't worry. Just because you can't see it easily doesn't mean that nothing's happening. Trust us—it is.

5. Recognize your role in the remodeling process and allow us to perform our work. Your input regarding design, expected craftsmanship, etc. will be incorporated into the job scope before the contract is signed. Once work is underway, give us the freedom to execute the job effectively. This is not to say that if you see something going wrong you shouldn't speak up. However don't try to take on our role in the process.

6. If possible, avoid making changes to the job scope. They tend to upset the schedule, which ultimately upsets you. If you do decide some changes are necessary settle the cost difference up front with the lead carpenter or salesperson so there is no misunderstanding.

Finally, remember that maintaining a good contractor-client relationship is a two-way street. Just as you would want others to respect your professional expertise, respect ours. At the same time, you can be sure that we're committed to providing you with as painless a remodel as possible, with the final results you expect!

9 From Exterior Porch to Interior Space

If you need additional living space and your home has a porch, you're in luck! Enclosing that porch could be a simple, cost-effective way to gain the space you want.

You can gain space without eliminating the yard and often, a portion of the structural work is already in place. Be sure that it will not detract from the style of your home. Enclosing a porch on some bungalows or Victorians could be a mistake if it destroys much of the home's sought-after charm.

Side porches can be easily converted into home offices, play rooms, or den/family rooms. Rear porches are ideal for adding space to extend your kitchen. With energy-efficient windows, any porch can be converted into a light-filled "Florida" room that's enclosed for year-round enjoyment.

Give us a call to talk about the work needed. The porch's location, its wall and floor materials, and the condition of the existing foundation will influence the ease or difficulty of modifying a porch. Your work may include:

- Insulating walls and ceilings. How much and the type of insulation used depends in part on the existing structure and the room's function.

- Adding or replacing windows with energy-efficient models. A professional can determine if window frames can be salvaged to reduce replacement costs. Remember to match or complement your home's existing window styles.

- Plumbing. The proximity of the room to existing plumbing will greatly impact the difficulty and cost of installing plumbing.

- Electrical wiring and fixtures. Build in all immediate and future electrical lines from the outset to avoid costly revisions later.

- Drywall, flooring, and millwork.

- Details such as door and window trim, chair railings, and moldings can make the difference between a room that looks finished—or one that simply looks like an enclosed porch.

- An important consideration is the heating and cooling system. While some homes may have systems that can accommodate additional rooms, others may need a supplement. Baseboard heating is an option. However, although it is easy to install, this type of heating is expensive to operate. Consider, also, a wood-burning stove. New models are efficient, attractive, and can heat a large room easily. We can help you decide how best to supply heating and cooling to your new space.

If you have a home with a porch and need additional space, you have all the ingredients you need to create a beautiful new room. What's keeping you from getting started?

10 Double Your Storage With Simple Creativity

One of the most common complaints we hear from our clients is lack of storage space. What they don't realize is that even owners of the smallest homes can double their storage space with some simple but creative modifications. Here are some ideas:

Kitchen
• Appliance garages—special cabinets with roll-down doors—can hide items like toasters, mixers, and food processors to free up counter space. Extra-deep counters also make a difference.

• Under-cabinet knife slats provide a protected spot to store utensils. Existing cabinets can be replaced with deeper or taller models that reach to the ceiling. Use the top shelves for rarely used items.

• Built-in refrigerators, perhaps faced with the same materials as your cabinets, can save space in a small kitchen.

• A separate pantry, which holds many items within easy reach, is another valuable storage space. Narrow, vertical areas can provide the perfect place to store mops and brooms.

• An island can improve traffic patterns in the kitchen while adding tons of storage. Slide-in cutting boards, pot racks, even an extra sink can be built in to make a big difference. Open shelves on one side can make food preparation quicker too.

Master Bedroom
• Under-the-bed rolling drawers can hold extra clothes or linens. A built-in cedar closet can keep your woolens safe from moths. This can be created from a portion of a current closet.

• Outfit your closet with double hanging rods, drawers, shoe holders, and hooks to create a space for everything.

Bedrooms, Living Rooms, or Dens
- Window seats and built-in book shelves can create a private nook while providing a place for books, toys, or linens.

Bathrooms
- Appliance garages work in the kitchen, so why not in the bathroom? A "garage" houses brushes, hair dryers, combs, and can include an electrical outlet, too. Medicine cabinets can be surface mounted or recessed between studs. Custom cabinetry affords optimal use of space. Vanity-to-ceiling and floor-to-ceiling built-ins that combine open shelves and enclosed cabinets are decorative as well as utilitarian.

- While standard height for most sinks is 30 to 32 inches, most adults can use a basin more comfortably when it's 34 to 38 inches high. This extra height allows for more storage; an extra shelf in the area below the basin and additional drawers on the sides.

Workshops or Garages
- Here, organization is very important. A place for everything and everything in its place can make a small space seem much more spacious. Pegboards can hold hooks for tools, paintbrushes, or just about anything. Accessories can be purchased to store small items like nails; some accessories hang right on the pegboard.

With a little creativity, your home can provide up to twice as much storage space as you're now using. For specific ideas for your home, give us a call. We're full of ingenuity!

Remodeling: Home as Art

Buying a remodeling project isn't like buying a car or dining room set. You can't simply compare prices and choose the one that requires the lowest investment. Because of the many types of home styles and the range of professionalism within the remodeling industry, there is no way to compare apples to apples. Apples to llamas is more like it. In fact, remodeling is probably as far from commodity buying as you can get.

But if we wanted to compare, we'd say that buying remodeling is most similar to buying artwork or graphic design work. Your home is a canvas with a painting already begun. We're the artists who will put our skills to work to finish the beautiful project.

Just like artists and graphic designers, each professional remodeler has a different creative mindset. If you were to talk to several remodelers, each would probably design a completely different solution to your problem.

And, just like artists, each remodeler has his or her own taste and skill level. It's really up to you, the homeowner, to find a remodeler that shares your vision for the final result. So think of your search for just the right remodeler as the search for an artist for your home. Here are some steps to follow:

- Begin by looking at the company's portfolio of completed projects. Ask how they created the solution to a particular remodeling problem.

- Don't rely on photography alone. Professional photography can make almost any project look wonderful. Take the time to visit a project or two to see the details up close. Often, the details are where the creative juices really shine.

- Talk to us about your budget and your vision for your project. Let us recommend the medium to use. Sculptures can be created out of clay, bronze, or gold, but do you really want to pay the price for gold? The artist may recommend bronze, which will provide the impact you want at a smaller investment.

• Let us be creative. After all, we spend our working lives designing projects that will help you make the most of the possibilities. Don't dictate the direction of the project. Suggest what you had in mind but let us demonstrate our skills.

• Remember, just like the more skilled and popular artists can command higher prices, you might be asked to invest a bit more for a remodeler who can deliver the best product and service.

• Become an educated consumer. People who invest in art don't spend their money until they've learned something about the topic. Then they feel comfortable spending their dollars on the best they can afford—even if it's only a pencil sketch.

Changing your home through remodeling can be one of the most rewarding decisions you'll ever make. Make the right choice, and you'll look at a masterpiece every time you open your door.

12 Remodeling Your Home for Your Golden Years

We have to face it—we're all growing older. Now, while aging is inevitable, it's not inevitable that we will be forced out of our homes when we become less active. With some careful planning, we can create a home that will continue to work well for us throughout our lives.

A home that's user-friendly for the elderly and the disabled doesn't have to look like a hospital. More and more products designed for disabled people have broken the "utilitarian" design mold and are now quite attractive. Plus, the simple structural modifications won't even be noticed. Here are some things to think about.

Make Things Easier to Reach
• Raise electrical outlets and phone jacks from 12 to 18 inches above the floor; people in wheelchairs will find this height more accesible.

• Lower electrical switches and thermostats from 48 to 42 inches from the floor; again, this provides easier access for people seated in wheelchairs.

• Move the bathroom medicine cabinet to the side of the bathroom vanity. Cabinets over the sink aren't practical.

• Have multiple light switches installed; for example—at the top and botttom of the stairs.

• Lower racks, shelves, and poles in closets to make them more accessible.

Make Moving Around Easier
• Widen doors from the standard 30 inches to 36 inches to accommodate a wheelchair.

• Install chair lifts or elevators if necessary to provide access to other levels of the house.

• Make sure the flooring in the kitchen and bath is made of a non-slip finish, and is in a matte tone to diminsh the glare of overhead lighting.

Make Things Easier to Use
• Replace standard door knobs with levers that are easier to maneuver with arthritic or disabled hands.

• Consider replacing double-hung or slider windows with crank-style casement windows.

• Install grab bars and railings (consider textured ones for a better grip) near the toilet and in the bath or shower stall.

• Use single-lever faucets with balled tips for the sink. These allow people to control the temperature with one lever.

• Make work areas easily distinguishable by using contrasting colors; this is especially important in the kitchen. This makes it easier for eyes that don't see quite as well. Install kitchen cabinets that feature roll-out drawers and easy-to-grip "C" or "D" handles.

• A flat glass-top stove is easy to clean, and makes it easier to remove pots and pans; make sure all appliance knobs are in the front.

• Don't overlook the world that remote controls have introduced. VCRs, CD players, garage door openers, touch-command lighting systems, ceiling fans, and even microwave ovens place the pleasures of everyday life at anyone's fingertips! And, a whole new world can be opened with the installation of voice-activated machinery.

Want more information on how to adapt your home? Give us a call.

YOUR MARKETING AND BUSINESS BOOKSHELF

Mastering the Business of Remodeling:
An Action Plan for Profit, Progress and Peace of Mind
Linda Case and Victoria Downing

Mastering the Business of Design/Build Remodeling
Linda Case, Victoria Downing, Wendy Jordan

The Remodelers Guide to Making and Managing Money:
*A Common-Sense Approach to Optimizing Compensation
and Profit*
Linda Case

The Guerrilla Marketing Books
Jay Conrad Levinson

Make Your Contacts Count: *Networking Know-How for Cash,
Clients, and Career Success*
Anne Baber, Lynne Waymon

Smart Networking: *How to Turn Contacts into Cash, Clients,
and Career Success*
Anne Baber, Lynne Waymon

Essential Books for Today's Remodeler:
THE PROFESSIONAL REMODELER'S LIBRARY

These books are designed and written to be of maximum benefit to the professional remodeler. They are quick and easy to read—just right for business owners with limited time.

TO ORDER,
by e-mail, visit **www.RemodelersAdvantage.com**
by phone us at **301-490-5620**
by fax complete the form below and fax to **301-498-6869**
by mail complete the form below and send it with payment to:

Remodelers Advantage Inc.
8504 Edenton Road
Fulton, MD 20759

Mail orders must be accompanied by check, money order or credit card number.

- ✂

QTY	TITLES	PRICE	TOTAL
_____	Mastering the Business of Design/Build Remodeling	$ 29.00	_____
_____	Mastering the Business of Remodeling	35.00	_____
_____	The Remodelers Guide to Making and Managing Money	27.00	_____

*SHIPPING/HANDLING

Subtotal	S/H
$ 0.00 to $29.99	$ 7.25
30.00 to 35.99	8.50
36.00 to 55.99	9.75
56.00 to 75.00	11.00

Subtotal _____

MD residents add 5% sales tax _____

*Shipping/Handling _____

TOTAL ENCLOSED _____

☐ Please charge my order: ☐ VISA ☐ MasterCard ☐ DISCOVER NOVUS ☐ AMERICAN EXPRESS Cards

Card # _____ Exp. Date _____

Name on Card _____ Signature _____

PROFESSIONAL SERVICES

REMODELERS ADVANTAGE helps remodeling contractors develop highly profitable, successful companies. We've worked with thousands of remodeling companies since 1982 helping them develop successful businesses with fast, practical, proven business solutions. With a thorough understanding of your challenges, we've designed our services exclusively for you, including:

BUSINESS CONSULTING: Our company is dedicated to the business side of remodeling. We spend our days talking to remodelers across the country about every kind of business issue that you can imagine. Since working with remodelers is all we do, there's no learning curve. You deserve to earn a better-than-average income, with a healthy net profit year after year without working more than 50 hours a week. It can be done and we can help you get there! If you want to improve your company's performance and maximize your results, talk to us about our consultation plans, including:

- Custom Strategic Business Analysis Consultation with on-site visit
- Ongoing Business Coaching

REMODELERS ADVANTAGE ROUNDTABLES, the national peer-review group for remodeling company owners. Why go it alone when you can fast track your progress along with a team of other remodeling company owners. This advisors group can help you gain greater profits and a business under control. Join today!

PERSONALITY PROFILING SERVICE: Our Personality Profiling service helps you hire and manage key employees. Hiring incorrectly can cost the company thousands of dollars in training and lost productivity. This tool can help you determine whether a person who appears so qualified, really is the right fit for the job. Plus, the information these tools uncover can improve your internal communications dramatically, resulting in happier employees and greater profits.

SEMINARS AND WORKSHOPS: If your organization is looking for innovative, informative educational programs for your members or customers, call today for information on the variety of seminars and workshops offered by nationally-known speakers.

For information on any of our services, visit
www.RemodelersAdvantage.com or call us at 301-490-5620